GU00360936

"I really enjoyed learning from all of
uted to this book. Every chapter is a
understanding, which will not only
ship, but stir up your heart too. What I liked most was the micro and
macro approach - where the writers give us the big picture, and then
help us think through how that all works out in the details of our
everyday lives, and in our gathered worship services. Great book!"
Matt Redman, worship leader and songwriter

"Why Worship is an invaluable and timely resource compiled by
two of the most thoughtful and experienced worship leaders in the
world. This is a book for everyone; for church leaders, for worship
leaders, and for anyone who ever wanted to discover the primary
purpose of their lives!"
Pete Greig, 24-7 Prayer International and Emmaus Rd churches.

"This is one of the most exciting, insightful and enlightening books
I've read on worship in a while. The anecdotes and exposition shared
paint a picture for me that'll help anyone reading see things not just
from Gods Perspective, but other people's too. This has never been so
important as the hidden fault lines in our relationships in the church
have become clear for the world to see. this book challenged me to
ask myself the question what the point was in having a great "glorious" time with God if it didn't affect how I lived. Prepare for a reboot
of your understanding."
Muyiwa Olarewaju OBE, worship leader and broadcaster

"What a wonderful book! Full of insight and inspiration, Why Worship is also catalyst for transformation. This diverse collection of
contributions from significant voices will undoubtedly stimulate our
thinking but, most of all, they lead us humbly again into the presence
of a holy but loving Heavenly Father."
Cathy Madavan, Speaker, writer and broadcaster

"My favourite thing about this book is the different perspectives on one main thing... Worship! Reading it provided much clarity on a word that is often misunderstood."
Guvna B, Rapper, Author & Broadcaster

"Engaging, biblical & inspiring. This wonderful book will help us all to understand and express our worship more fully."
Gavin Calver, CEO Evangelical Alliance

"As I started reading this glorious book, I could feel my heart alive with hope, as we as Gods people fight for clarity in an increasingly messy world. THANKYOU to Tim and Nick and all who have shared their legacy stories of truthful worth ship... for as we continue to dive deep into this realm, as the spirit of God asks us to Come Up Here... together we will continue to witness the rise and rise of Gods glory. To the praise of His most Holy name."
Darlene Zschech, worship leader and singer-songwriter

WHY WORSHIP?

Liza Hoeksma works in communications for Soul Survivor Watford church, as well as being a freelance writer and editor. She has worked on a number of books with others including Mike Pilavachi, Andy Croft and Ali Martin from Soul Survivor; Patrick Regan from Kintsugi Hope, and Tich & Joan Smith from LIV Village in South Africa.

WHY WORSHIP?

Insights into the Wonder of Worship

TIM HUGHES,
DR NICK DRAKE
AND LIZA HOEKSMA

First published in Great Britain in 2021

Society for Promoting Christian Knowledge
36 Causton Street
London SW1P 4ST
www.spck.org.uk

Copyright © Spring Harvest 2021

All rights reserved. No part of this book may be reproduced or transmitted in any form or by any means, electronic or mechanical, including photocopying, recording, or by any information storage and retrieval system, without permission in writing from the publisher.

SPCK does not necessarily endorse the individual views contained in its publications.

British Library Cataloguing-in-Publication Data
A catalogue record for this book is available from the British Library

ISBN 978-0-281-08575-0
eBook ISBN 978-0-281-08610-8

1 3 5 7 9 10 8 6 4 2

Typeset by Nord Compo

First printed in Great Britain by Ashford Colour Press

eBook by Nord Compo

Produced on paper from sustainable forests

Contents

Contents

Part 3
WHAT HAPPENS
WHEN WE WORSHIP?

Part 4
THE FUTURE

Introduction

DR NICK DRAKE

If there is a 'key' to life, a secret that unlocks the door to living the best life possible, it's the key of worship. Right worship, of the right thing, leads to the right life.

Worship has become a narrow word for church music when it should be a broad word meaning a life lived for the One who creates, sustains and perfects all things. My invitation to you, therefore, is to see this book in your hands as a journey deeper into life itself – how do we *worship better*? How can we honour, love and serve God better? How can our lives be more aligned to his incredible life?

For all of us involved in writing this book, pursuing a life of worship has been key for us personally. It has been a source of great delight and strength: an activity, a discipline and a joy that has become central to who we are. Our hope is that what we have put down on paper – our passion for seeing Jesus glorified, praised and adored here on earth as he is in heaven – carries over to you. We pray that as you read this book, you won't just gain information but will receive transformation by God's Spirit that fuels your own personal life of worship and makes you a fervent champion of worship in your local church and community.

This book was written against the backdrop of the Covid-19 pandemic, a time we couldn't gather together for much of the year, and when we could, we weren't allowed to raise our voices together in song. Though it was a devastating time, these restrictions reminded us again about the heart of worship. There will be times in all our lives when we can't sing or raise our hands or stand in worship – perhaps due to a short-term illness, perhaps because of longer-term physical impairments– but when we're faced with these times, we refocus and remind ourselves that those things aren't the whole story of worship. Worship is so much more, as we will explore in these pages.

The power of this book lies in the fact that it is a collection of voices. We wanted a book that contained many different perspectives on the one central, glorious reality of worshipping God. In Revelation, Chapters 4 and 5, John experiences heavenly reality and sees an incredible vision of true worship. Each chapter in this book is like a different snapshot of a worship scene like this. It's as if we've handed each author a disposable camera, like people used to do at weddings, and invited them to share with us what they saw through that lens. These different perspectives together make up a collage far greater than any one of us could write on our own. They provide a multi-layered picture of what it means to worship God.

Each author has been picked for either their experience as a worship leader or expertise as a theologian or pastor in a particular area to do with worship. Most have links to Spring Harvest – an annual Christian festival here in the UK – and you will be very familiar with some, while less so with some others. We highly recommend each of them to you. Sit under their feet and ask God to stir your heart and teach you new things about worshipping him.

All of the content in the book was curated by me and Tim. We have both been worship leaders for most of our lives and, more recently, we have been running – together with Tim's wife Rachel and a wider team – a new church called Gas Street Church in the centre of Birmingham, UK. One of our key values as a church is that everything we do should be 'woven in worship', so it seems fitting that we oversee a book such as this one now in your hands. In compiling the content, we found ourselves personally challenged, encouraged and inspired to travel further down the life's journey of being a worshipper and leading others to worship. We hope you will too.

How to use this book

The book is divided into three sections: in Part 1, we look at who we worship and why we worship; Part 2 focuses on where and how we worship and Part 3 focuses on what happens when we worship. To close, we look to the future – both the glimpse of eternity we get in Revelation and what we believe God is saying to the Church about worship today. There is so much to learn from and be inspired by within each section. At the start of each part, I will introduce the main themes and locate the section within the bigger map of the journey of the book. There is a logic and flow to how the whole book has been curated if you'd like to read it from beginning to end, but it's also the kind of book that works to dip into a chapter at a time, in almost any order, as they each stand alone. Need a quick insight into the power of praise? Read Noel Robinson's Chapter 9. Want to study the centrality of Christ to worship in Hebrews? Jump into Dr Helen Morris's Chapter 3, and so on. Our hope is that this book is a companion for you for years to come and stays close at hand as a useful and inspiring resource.

Before you turn the page and start Part 1, why not take a moment to grab a pen to make some notes and to pray. Come to the text *expectant* that God wants to speak to you.

Come Holy Spirit. Be with me as I read this book. Speak to me and make the truths contained here alive and real in my life. I'm here not just for information about you, but to be moved closer in my relationship with you, that I may be someone who worships you in spirit and in truth and displays your likeness to those I meet.

Amen.

Part I

WHO AND WHY
WE WORSHIP

Let me introduce Part 1 – who and why we worship. This section opens with Tim writing on the 'why' of worship. Reflecting on Romans 12.1, Tim encourages us to see worship foundationally as a whole-of-life response to the God who has poured out his love to us through the cross. He then moves on to suggest we're not only invited to worship as a thankful response, but we're *created* to worship. Worship is something deep in our very DNA – we find out not only who we are, but what we're living for when we worship our Creator and Saviour rather than any created thing.

We then move into three further chapters that each reflect on the 'who' of worship: one God who is triune in his nature – Father, Son and Holy Spirit. Theologians argue that questions about the nature of worship are actually questions about the nature of God, and so it's crucial to start a study of worship by studying God himself, as revealed by the Holy Spirit through the Biblical text. A trinitarian understanding of God, after all, is actually what *defines* our worship as Christian.

Dr John Andrews begins with a fantastic detailed study of the 'Shema', the Jewish confession of faith that we find in Deuteronomy 6.4–5: 'Hear, O Israel: The Lord our God, the Lord is one. And you shall love the Lord your God with all your heart and with all your soul and with all your might.' This is a foundational revelation of the nature of the Oneness of God and our right response to him. He explores what it meant for the people of God at that time, and for us today, to not only hear this truth of God's nature but to obey it.

He writes, 'If we are to authentically live out a lifestyle of worship it must come from truth we have heard about him and a revelation we have received from him.'

We then move on to explore the absolute centrality of Jesus to our worship through the book of Hebrews with Dr Helen Morris. Hebrews is a key text, if not *the* key text, for understanding Christian worship. It is so rich with imagery and Old Testament reference, however, that it can be hard to understand sometimes. Helen does a fantastic job in making clear from the text a vision of Jesus and his absolute unrivalled uniqueness. She writes, 'In Hebrews, the author expresses his praise to Jesus by presenting the amazing truths about who Jesus is and what he has done, with beauty and intricacy.' In this chapter, we are reawakened to the beauty of who Jesus is and the majestic scope of what he has done for us on the cross.

Finally, Part 1 ends with my own chapter on the work of the Holy Spirit in worship. Both personally and theologically, I am passionate about the centrality of the Spirit to Christian life and worship, and so I wanted to write a chapter that would inspire and provoke you, as you read, to partner further with the work of the Spirit in your life. The theme of the Holy Spirit in worship has often, unfortunately, been sidelined as a 'Pentecostal-Charismatic concern', but in this chapter, I explain how all true Christian worship is Spirit-led and Spirit-filled. The Holy Spirit plays a pivotal role in relating us to the Father and the Son and in making real to us the work of the Father through the Son on the cross. We explore how the Holy Spirit glorifies Jesus through our worship, establishes our identity and resources our response.

DR NICK DRAKE

1

Why worship?

TIM HUGHES

Tim and his wife, Rachel, are lead pastors at Gas Street in Birmingham, a church they planted in 2015 in the heart of the UK's second biggest city. Tim has been a worship leader for many years, writing songs such as 'Here I Am To Worship' and 'Happy Day', as well as pioneering a ministry called 'Worship Central' that exists to equip and train worship leaders and teams around the world.

It was a cold and grey Sunday morning in October. I was up early, had gulped down a caffeine fix, sound checked and rehearsed; now I was ready to lead the church in worship. The band exploded into life, and we began to sing our first song. As I surveyed the sea of faces in front of me, I noticed an enthusiastic worshipper walking to the front of the church. He was wearing a white shirt, cream chinos, and – in a surprising fashion statement – he had a white towel wrapped around his waist.

As the air filled with the congregation's praise, the man (now standing right before me) began to casually unbutton his shirt as if it were the most natural thing in the world. I looked around, but people were either fixated on the giant screen at the front displaying the song words or had their eyes firmly closed. No one other than me seemed to notice that there was now a semi-naked man singing his heart out at the front of church. A serious panic began to grow in me. I'd never read the book on what to do if you're leading worship and someone starts stripping in front of you. I carried on singing, blindly hoping he would get dressed and go back to his seat, but instead he began to slowly unbutton his trousers. Good Lord!

I stepped away from the microphone and sent panicked signals to one of the leaders of the church by the side of the stage. When I shouted, 'Help! There's a man getting naked in church!' it certainly got their attention. They quickly rushed over and began to engage the man in conversation, politely inviting him to go outside to chat more. He was having none of it. After many futile attempts at removing him peacefully, they realized he wasn't going anywhere without a fight. While they began to drag him away, he kept trying to pull his trousers down, leaving them trying to pull them back up! Of course, more people in the congregation had noticed by now and were somewhat distracted from their worship. But, like the string quartet dutifully playing while the Titanic sank, I faithfully soldiered on singing, 'Isn't he beautiful. Beautiful, isn't he!'

Moments like that remind us that life is messy and broken; things don't always go how we plan. So what does worship look like in the reality of life's twists and turns? What does it look like in the everyday? Not the once-a-year, perfect encounters at a festival but the day in, day out, week in, week out? The times when we're sitting in church, thinking, *What on earth am I doing here? Why do we sing these songs? What does it actually mean to worship? What difference does this all make? How could this motley crew of a congregation ever hope to have an impact in our towns and cities?* (I, of course, never think that about my church . . . I only say it in case you do about yours!) And, amazingly, God is okay with us asking these questions. Worship is about the mess and fragility of humanity being caught up in the perfection and love of divinity. It's about an encounter, not rules, religion or regulations. We miss the point when we reduce worship to programmes and practicalities, rather than focusing on the person and presence of Jesus. It's about relationship. And, of course, this relationship weaves through the whole tapestry of our lives. This is the way the Apostle Paul explains what worship is in the book of Romans:

So here's what I want you to do, God helping you: Take your everyday, ordinary life – your sleeping, eating, going-to-work, and walking-around life – and place it before God as an offering. Embracing what God does for you is the best thing you can do for him. (Romans 12.1, MSG)

In worship, we bring everything – our normal, mundane, and everyday musings; our hopes and dreams; our money and resources; our relationships and careers; our physical bodies and emotions; our strengths and weaknesses – and we place them all before God in an offering of surrender. We are saying, 'I am completely yours.' We don't do this out of a noble sense of duty, rather as a response to God's initiating and unconditional love. The NIV translates the start of those words of Paul's as, '*In view of God's mercy* offer your bodies as a living sacrifice' (italics added). Worship is a response to an encounter with God's lavish love and mercy. One of the most beautiful descriptions of worship is that it's 'an attempt to cope with the abundance of God's love'.[1] Worship overflows and pours out of us when we understand the wonder of who God is. We love because God first loved us (1 John 4.19).

And we're all invited. Every single one of us. Jesus made that really clear in his encounter with a Samaritan woman at a well that we read about in John 4. As a Jewish rabbi, Jesus would have been expected to give a Samaritan – a woman, and someone who had made her moral choices (she'd had five husbands and was currently living with another man) – a wide berth. She was a social outcast. Instead, he engaged her in conversation and redefined the geography of worship.

No longer is worship to be limited to temples, techniques and traditions. Rather, as Jesus explained, 'a time is coming when you

---

1 David F. Ford and Daniel W. Hardy, *Living in Praise*, Dayton, Longman & Todd Ltd, 2005, 2.

will worship the Father neither on this mountain nor in Jerusalem' (John 4.21). Instead, 'worshipers must worship in the Spirit and in truth.'

The centre point of worship was no longer to be found in a temple building made of stone in Jerusalem. It would be – and still is – found in the person of Christ. In Jesus, through the power of the Holy Spirit, we can now experience the presence of the Father. In worship, we can now boldly draw near to God, knowing that he will draw near to us (James 4.8).

Created to worship

We're not just *invited* to worship, we're *created* to worship. The Westminster catechism is a document written to teach doctrine to the masses, and is framed around a number of questions and responses. One of the fundamental questions it asks is 'What is the chief end of humankind?' It answers by saying, 'the chief end of humankind is to glorify God and enjoy him forever.' Let's break that down. Our purpose in life is to glorify God. Take a look at some of these verses about worship:

But you are a chosen people, a royal priesthood, a holy nation, God's special possession, that you may declare the praises of him who called you out of darkness into his wonderful light. (1 Peter 2.9)

In Christ we have also obtained an inheritance, having been destined according to the purpose of him who accomplishes all things according to his counsel and will, so that we, who were the first to set our hope on Christ, might live for the praise of his glory.
(Ephesians 1.11–12, NSRV)

> 'Teacher, which is the greatest commandment in the Law?'
> Jesus replied: 'Love the Lord your God with all your heart and
> with all your soul and with all your mind.'
> (Matthew 22.36–37)

We have been chosen and called in order to declare God's praise.
We have been created for God's glory, so worship is central to our
existence. Jesus told us that loving God with everything we have is
the most important thing we can ever do.

Our ultimate purpose in life is found in bringing glory to God.
You only have to take a quick look at the Bible to see just how profound the call to worship is:

When Abraham first encountered God, he was called to obedient sacrifice, an act of worship (Genesis 12.7). When Moses led the
people out of Egypt, it was so that they could worship the Lord,
and Miriam led them in a song of worship (Exodus 3.12; 15.1–18).
When Hannah handed over her much longed-for baby son, Samuel,
to the Lord, she lifted up her voice to worship (1 Samuel 2.1–10).
When David danced before the Lord with all his might, it was
an act of worship (2 Samuel 6.14). When Elijah called down fire
from heaven on Mount Carmel, it was in the context of worship
(1 Kings 18.39). When Job lost everything, he fell to his knees in
worship (Job 1.20). When Mary discovered that she was carrying
Jesus Christ, the Saviour of the world, in her womb, she worshipped
(Luke 1.46–55). When the wise men greeted the Christ child, they
worshipped (Matthew 2.11). When Simeon was presented with the
infant Christ in the temple, he worshipped (Luke 2.28). When the
disciples realized that Jesus Christ is the Lord, the Messiah, they
worshipped (Matthew 14.33). And when the twenty four elders, the
four living creatures, the multitudes of angels and every creature
in heaven and earth see Jesus, the Lamb that was slain, standing in
the centre of the throne in heaven, they lift up their voices and worship (Revelation 4 and 5).

Let's be clear. God doesn't command or create us to worship because he's a needy, sycophantic and insecure divine being. He's not desperately lonely, seeking affirmation and love to make him feel better. He is perfect in every way, the eternal triune God. God the Father, God the Son and God the Holy Spirit live in perfect unity and love. God is complete. But it's out of his abundance and goodness that he created humankind to experience and know the depths of his love. Jesus laid aside his majesty, taking on the nature of a servant, and walked upon the earth that he had created and spoken into being. Why? Jesus himself said, 'I have come that they may have life, and have it to the full' (John 10.10). God wants us to experience the great joy of knowing him, the extravagant life and blessing that is found in relationship with him. It's in worship, by putting God first in our lives, that we discover true life, freedom and joy.

Remember the chief end of humankind is to glorify God *and* enjoy him forever. As C.S. Lewis reflects, 'In commanding us to glorify him, God is inviting us to enjoy him.'[2]

To know and be known by God is the greatest thing that can happen to a mere mortal. We worship God because he is all-deserving, all-powerful and worthy of the adoration of heaven and earth. But as we worship, we find we encounter blessing upon blessing.

The truth is *everybody worships something*. If something captivates our heart's affection, our mind's attention and our soul's ambition, it effectively has our worship – be it a relationship, money, success or power. However, few of these experiences or objects of affection bring any sense of completion or lasting contentment. You may have all the money in the world, every earthly possession you desire and still be left feeling empty and lost. Until we discover our purpose in God, we will never be satisfied. St Augustine once prayed, 'You have made us for yourself, O Lord, and our

2   C.S. Lewis, *Reflections on the Psalms*, New York: Harcourt, Brace & Co., 1958, 97.

hearts are restless until they rest in you.' In Jesus, we find the answer to the meaning of life. We have been made by the Maker and saved by the Saviour with the one extraordinary purpose of glorifying God.

Task vs gift

The theologian James Torrance speaks about two different responses in worship: *task* and *gift*. Many of us can view worship as something we simply do – a task. We attend church, we pray, we read the Bible, we give our money, we serve the poor, we give, give, give. This view of worship not only places ourselves at the centre of worship, but also leads to exhaustion and burnout. In our own efforts, we can never do enough.

The other perspective of worship is as a gift. Worship is something we are invited into. In worship, we experience God's presence and are gathered up into the community of God the Father, God the Son and God the Holy Spirit. When we understand worship as time in God's presence, we discover that in worship, we are encouraged, envisioned, inspired, restored, replenished, renewed, healed and set free. Worship becomes life-changing and exhilarating. It is our great joy in life.

When I was eleven years old, I attended a New Wine Bible conference. I'll never forget that first meeting. My father was a vicar so I had grown up going to church, but nothing prepared me for that first time of worship and teaching. There was a band on the stage playing simple songs with passion and exuberance. All around, people were singing as if this was the most important activity they would ever be involved in. Some had their hands in the air, others were weeping, many had their eyes closed.

For perhaps the first time in my life, I felt close to God. It struck me immediately that they weren't singing about a God they had read about; they were singing to a God they knew. Something in me broke, and at the end of the meeting I asked someone to pray for me, that I too would know God. That moment changed me forever. My priorities shifted; my sole purpose became to follow God. On returning from that week, I started learning how to play the guitar. My goal wasn't to become the next Jimi Hendrix; my deep desire was to be able to worship God in the privacy of my room. I would spend hours just singing out and enjoying God's presence. It was during those moments of worship, alongside studying the Scriptures, that I learnt about God's heart and his ways. It was during these God encounters, on my own, in my room, that God shaped me for so much of what I now spend my days on. It was in worship that God brought healing to my heart, he instilled a courage in my bones, he put a joy in my very being.

The power of gathering

Jesus who is perfect in every way, from everlasting to everlasting, is the one person we can wholeheartedly depend on. He won't disappoint or turn us away. Rather, in his presence everything begins to make sense. That's why worship is the most important activity we could ever engage in. And, of course, it involves a relationship that impacts every part of our lives, but we also see throughout the Scriptures that something profound and mysterious happens when the people of God gather together to sing.

Many times the Bible tells us to 'sing to the Lord'. From showers to stadiums, cars to concerts, there is something powerful about singing. It engages more than our minds; it engages our whole physicality. We see many moments where the people of Israel, the early church, gathered together in worship to sing. Skip to the end of the Bible, in the book of Revelation,[3] we catch a glimpse of what we will spend eternity doing.

---

3   We'll go on to explore this in greater detail in Chapter 11.

Then I looked, and I heard the voice of many angels surrounding the throne and the living creatures and the elders; they numbered myriads of myriads and thousands of thousands, *singing* with full voice,
'Worthy is the Lamb that was slaughtered
to receive power and wealth and wisdom and might
and honor and glory and blessing!'
Then I heard every creature in heaven and on earth and under the earth and in the sea, and all that is in them, *singing*,
'To the one seated on the throne and to the Lamb
be blessing and honor and glory and might
forever and ever!'
And the four living creatures said, 'Amen!' And the elders fell down and worshiped.
(Revelation 5.11–14, italics added)

Singing is clearly an important element to our expression of worship. It unites us as the Church, it inspires us and strengthens us and, wonderfully, God chooses to inhabit our gatherings as we lift up our praise (Psalm 22.3, KJV). Our gathered expressions of worship, overflowing out of a lifestyle of worship, are powerful. More powerful than perhaps we give them credit.

A number of years ago, at the end of a time of worship, someone came up to ask me what had been going on during the singing. I did a double take as it was a Hollywood celebrity. It turned out he was at a low ebb in his life and a friend had bought him along to church. He kept saying, 'I just wept my way through the worship. What was that? I've never experienced anything like that before.' I explained that he was experiencing the love of God as the Spirit was moving in his heart. In the eyes of the world, he had everything – success, money, adulation – but it all paled into insignificance compared to experiencing the love of God. I've no idea how that encounter went on to shape him, but as a pastor I've lost count of the number of times people visiting church for the first time have bawled their way through the worship. Each time, the question they ask is 'What was that?' What they are experiencing is not sensational music or songs; they are being touched by the presence and love of God. Over the years, I've seen many come to faith in the context of worship, people being miraculously healed and many being strengthened and encouraged to keep going. Something significant happens when the people of God join together in praise and worship.

Worship is a weapon

We get an incredible insight into the power of worship in 2 Chronicles 20. It was a dark and terrifying moment for the people of Judah; a vast army was approaching with the sole intent of inflicting mass destruction. Humanly speaking, this looked like game over for Judah. Alarmed, King Jehoshaphat called all the people of Judah together, proclaiming a fast. As they gathered, Jehoshaphat led them in worship. 'Oh Lord, God of our fathers, are you not the God who is heaven? You rule over all the kingdoms of the nations. Power and might are in your hand and no-one can withstand you' (2 Chronicles 20.6).

In a moment of crisis, rather than filling their minds with the frightening possibilities that lay ahead, they filled their hearts and minds with the truth of who God is. A mighty and powerful king who rules and reigns over all the nations. They chose faith over fear. Trust over terror. And as they punctuated the air with praise, God began to move. The Spirit of the Lord fell upon one of the leaders, Jehaziel, and he spoke God's word directly into the situation: 'Do not be afraid or discouraged because of this vast army. For the battle is not yours but God's . . . Take up your positions; stand firm and see the deliverance the Lord will give you' (2 Chronicles 20.15–17).

Confident that God was in control and at work, Jehoshaphat made a bold decision. He appointed singers and musicians to stand at the front of the army, commanding them to 'sing to the Lord and to praise him for the splendour of his holiness' (v. 21). Can you imagine the sight? A vast and vicious enemy army fast approaching, ready to kill and destroy, and what did the people of Judah do? They began to sing, 'Give thanks to the Lord for his love endures forever.' It makes no sense. This is serious life-and-death stuff, but at the front of Judah's army was a choir singing in four-part harmony!

As they sang, the Lord set ambushes against the various enemy armies, and they began to turn on one another. Rather than destroying the people of Judah, they began killing each other. And all while the sound of praise filled the battlefield. Eventually, the men of Judah looked out to see the enemy army, now completely defeated, lying dead on the ground. The greatest military victory in the history of Judah and they had done absolutely nothing . . . except worship!

Worship is a weapon. Later in this book, we've dedicated a whole chapter to looking at the power of praise. It is the most dynamic and powerful thing that the church engages in. When we worship, God moves. When we worship, strongholds break, circumstances shift, lives are changed. In worship, we proclaim Jesus is Lord. Lord over everything. Over every threat that might come our way . . . sickness, accusation, hardship, confusion . . . Jesus rules and reigns above it all. On the cross and through the resurrection, Jesus defeated not only our sin, but also death. As followers of Christ, we are on the winning team! With great boldness, Paul taunts the enemy, saying:

> Death has been swallowed up in victory.
> Where, O death, is your victory?
> Where, O death, is your sting?
> Thanks be to God! He gives us victory through our Lord Jesus Christ.
> (1 Corinthians 15.54)

In worship, we align ourselves with Christ's victory. We remind ourselves that the same power that raised Jesus from the grave lives in us. Us! Every time we sing, pray, give, gather in church, put God first in our relationships and workplace, and choose to live in the opposite spirit to the current age, we usher in this victory. In worship, we are empowered. We step into our great purpose, and everything begins to make sense.

When we worship, we can be filled with joy no matter what our circumstances are. We can find reason to hope even when all around us seems bleak. We can be perplexed without being in despair and rejoice even in sorrow. Dutch author Corrie Ten Boom knew what it was like to face extreme suffering and loss, having been a prisoner in the barbaric Ravensbruck concentration camp during the Second World War. She writes, 'If you look at the world, you'll be distressed. If you look within, you'll be depressed. If you look at God, you'll be at rest.'

In worship, we come before God with all our hang-ups, fears and mess, aware of our finite nature, and we embrace God's infinite power, his unending love, his might, strength and peace. We worship God because we've been created for this very purpose and, in doing so, we come alive.

Worship is so much more than a few songs sung in church on a Sunday. Worship is a relationship with the God of heaven and earth that shifts and shapes everything about us. The great American author A. W. Tozer wrote, 'What comes into our minds when we think about God is the most important thing about us.'[4] If worshipping God fails to inspire or excite us, could it be that we're not seeing correctly? We're not grasping the enormity of who God truly is. As Matt Redman writes, 'when we face up to the glory of God, we find ourselves face down in worship.'[5]

Our hope and prayer is that through the pages of this book you might begin to understand just how extraordinary the Lord God

4 A. W. Tozer, *The Knowledge of the Holy*, Harper Collins, 1961, 1.

5 Matt Redman, *Facedown*, Kingsway Communications Ltd, 2004, 17.

Almighty is and begin to catch a vision for what a life of worship might look like. If that happens, you'll never be the same again!

Further resources for digging deeper

A. W. Tozer – *The Knowledge of the Holy*

A. W. Tozer – *Whatever Happened to Worship?*

David Peterson – *Engaging with God*

James B. Torrance – *Worship, Community and the Triune God of Grace*

<Worshipcentral.org> – For lots of resources, talks and input on worship, head to the Worship Central website.

2

Who we worship:
the Lord who is one

DR JOHN ANDREWS

John has been in full-time church leadership in the UK for over 30 years. He also holds a Masters degree in Pentecostal and Charismatic Studies from Sheffield University and a doctorate from the University of Wales. He has authored 13 books, including Extravagant – When Worship Becomes Lifestyle. *Born in Belfast, Northern Ireland, John has ministered in over 30 nations of the world with a passion to equip and inspire leaders as well as empower followers of Jesus into effective lifestyle and service.*

The Shema: 'Hear, O Israel: The LORD our God, the LORD is one. And you shall love the LORD your God with all your heart and with all your soul and with all your might' (Deuteronomy 6.4–5).

Within the opening lines of the Shema (the Jewish confession of faith that we read in Deuteronomy 6.4–5) are two vital ingredients at the heart of all true worship: a revelation of who God is and a response to him on the basis of that revelation. Though the Shema stretches over three separate passages of the Torah, it is this opening statement that captures the very essence of the heart-agreement the Lord wanted to establish with his people.[1] As they were about to enter the land promised by God, Moses brought these new words to them, words that were intended to become the bedrock of their confession and conduct, their worship and their walk.

---

1 Deuteronomy 6.4–9, 11.13–21 and Numbers 15.37–41. The reciting of these passages, Keri'at Shema, framed the basis of morning and evening prayers.

The Shema gets its name from the first word of the confession: *šāma'* ('hear'). Although the word can simply mean to hear a noise or voice, in the Hebrew Scriptures it is also used in a variety of ways highlighting its depth and wealth. It's an important word in Deuteronomy, with its root appearing in one form or another 92 times in the text, and it can be no coincidence that in a book known to the Jewish people as *D'varim* (meaning 'words'), the word *shema* (hear) features so heavily. In this context, as in many others throughout the Scriptures, to hear does not simply mean to listen, but rather to listen *and obey*. Thus, obedience is the evidence of our hearing. In this context, if I do not do, it is because I have not heard.

Jesus tells the story of a father who had two sons. The father asked his first son to do something to which he responded, 'I will not', but later on he did it. To the second son he made the same request, to which he answered, 'I will, sir', but he did not do what the father asked. In this context the first son *heard*,[2] and this might explain why so often Jesus said to his listeners, 'he who has ears, let him hear.'[3] Every parent has surely experienced the reality of *shema*, when our children have listened to our words but not heard them!

With no verb 'to obey' in biblical Hebrew, the word *šāma'* helped form a foundational and transformational idea within the Scriptures that if we truly heard, we would obey. Therefore, to hear in this way must be central in our relationship with the Lord, and it is essential if worship is to become a lifestyle, proclaimed through our words and demonstrated through our actions. What we hear will determine the focus of our worship, and how we hear will determine the scope of our worship.

As Rabbi Sacks explained, '*Shema Yisrael* does not mean "Hear, O Israel." It means something like, "Listen. Concentrate. Give the word of God your most focused attention. Strive to understand. Engage all

---

2   Matthew 21.28–32.

3   Matthew 13.9, 43.

your faculties, intellectual and emotional. Make his will your own."
For what he commands you to do is not irrational or arbitrary but
for your welfare, the welfare of your people, and ultimately for the
benefit of all humanity.'[4]

It is interesting that when the Lord asked Solomon what he wanted
as he became king, he did not specifically ask for wisdom but rather
he asked for 'a listening heart' (*lev shomeah*).[5] A life that honours the
unrivalled Lord is one where a listening, hearing heart beats within,
for a hearing heart will lead to a life that is holy.

What makes our hearts more prone to hear?

Hunger for the Lord

'I seek you with all my *heart*; do not let me stray from your
commands' (Psalm 119.10).

Humility before the Lord

'I have hidden your word in my *heart* that I might not sin against
you' (Psalm 119.11).

Honesty with the Lord

'Create in me a pure *heart*, O God, and renew a steadfast spirit within me' (Psalm 51.10).

Not only will hunger, humility and honesty help guard our hearts
and keep them sensitive to the presence of the Lord, but these three
qualities are deeply attractive to him, for he feeds hunger, lifts
humility and responds to honesty.

---

4   Rabbi Jonathan Sacks, *Covenant & Conversation: Deuteronomy: Renewal of the Sinai Covenant*, Maggid Books, 2019, 68–69.

5   1 Kings 3.9 – In 2 Chronicles 1.10 he asked for 'wisdom and knowledge'.

What does the Lord want us to hear? He wants us to *hear a revelation* of who he is:

'the LORD our God, the LORD is One.'

He wants us to *hear a response* of what he desires from us, in the light of that revelation:

'And you shall love the LORD your God with all your heart, and with all your soul and with all your strength.'

So let's look a little closer at the revelation and response.

Hear the revelation

'the LORD our God, the LORD is One.'

This little phrase packs so much in just a few words. From this, Israel was reminded of three facts:

He is God – he who made creation

'In the beginning *God created* the heavens and the earth' (Genesis 1.1).

He is Lord – he who entered into covenant with them

'*The LORD said* to Abram . . . ' (Genesis 12.1).

He is one – he who stands alone

'There is none like you, O LORD; you are great, and your name is great in might' (Jeremiah 10.6).

If we go with the translation 'the LORD our God, the LORD is one' (ESV), then we see something of the unrivalled nature of the Lord captured in this word. The Hebrew word for one is *'eḥāḏ*, and although it points to the number one, it can, in certain contexts, point to uniqueness and being first above all. See how Zechariah used it in this very sense when he declared, 'And the Lord will be king over all the earth. On that day the Lord will be *one* and his name *one*' (Zechariah 14.9, italics added).

The Shema called the people to hear who the Lord was, and to understand that the one they had entered into a relationship with was before all, above all and beyond all. Having left Egypt with its many gods, they were about to enter a land filled with names that would attempt to rival his, but through this confession and this revelation, they were reminded that the God who made the world had no rivals and that the Lord who made an agreement with them stood alone, apart and above! He is one . . . he is God alone!

If we are to authentically live out a lifestyle of worship, it must come from truth we have heard about him and a revelation we have received from him. Our hearing cannot be based on what others have heard and passed on to us second-hand, but must come from what our own hearts have heard. Our seeing cannot be a description of what others have seen, but must come from what the eyes of our own hearts have seen. Information about God is not always the same as revelation of God. Information will exercise our intellect, but revelation will transform our world view.

If we know – if we have heard and seen – that 'the Lord our God, the Lord is one', then everything changes. We will see him not as one of many, but as one alone. We will see the agreement he has made with us in Christ Jesus through the lens of grace, generosity, goodness and love. We will understand that we are a privileged people and with that privilege and position comes gloriously heavy responsibility. We will live our lives in service to him knowing that anything else, no matter how good it is, is insufficient, and inadequate in comparison. If the revelation that he is unrivalled truly resides in our hearts, that he is before all, above all and alone, then our only response can be wholehearted surrender and willing service.

Hear the response

The Shema continues:

'And you shall love the LORD your God with all your heart and with all your soul and with all your strength.'

From the revelation that he is one/alone, a response is encouraged that has within it five dynamic ideas worthy of our consideration.

From command to response

'*And* you shall love . . . '

The inclusion or exclusion of just one word in the way this phrase is translated can make a huge difference as to how we hear what the Lord is asking for. When the word 'and' is excluded, the Shema becomes a command from God, but when 'and' is included, the Shema becomes a response to God. The phrase used in the original Hebrew is *ve'ahavta* and literally could read, '*and* you shall love', which seems to make greater sense in the light of what has gone before. Having *heard* that the 'Lord our God the Lord is one, unique, unrivalled and alone', surely what comes next must be a response to that truth . . . '*and*'. Love cannot be demanded nor commanded, but rather it must come from a heart free to hear and choose. Worship cannot be forced or coerced and should come from a heart that expresses in words and actions the revelation it has truly heard.

True, authentic worship cannot be manipulated or manufactured, but is created out of what we hear and see for ourselves. We cannot worship from another's wonder, and we must not succumb to the pressure of peers nor the folly of fake praise. The Shema is not merely a command, but a response, for the Lord desires that our worship comes from faith not fear, from authenticity not pretence and from revelation not information. That's why 'and' is vital, because our 'and' connects revelation to response!

From feeling to knowing

'And *you shall love . . .* '

The phrase 'And you shall love . . . ' in English comes from one word in the Hebrew Bible, namely *ve'ahavta*, and it contains the verb to love, *'āhaḇ*. Though feelings are not excluded from the many nuances within the word, this love runs deeper than our feelings and goes beyond our emotions. In fact, to love in this way doesn't require feelings and emotion; they are a bonus feature to the main heartbeat of the word. To love is to act lovingly towards someone or something and to be focused, faithful and loyal. Love is not about what I feel, but about what I do. Love is less about emotion and more about action. Whatever or whomever I love will be evidenced in the way I behave towards that thing or person.

Words are easy to learn and rehearse, but actions are harder to fake in the long run. How we act towards the Lord is the true indicator of our love for him, and though words are a vitally important aspect of our faith, if our actions are true, words are not always required. Though the Shema contains some of the greatest words ever penned, it is more than words to be learned and more than poetic literature to be enjoyed, for the Shema is a call to worship as demonstrated in our behaviour. According to the Shema, when it comes to worship, actions speak louder than words!

From fringe to centre

'with *all your heart . . .* '

When it comes to the heart, we must be careful not to be distracted by biological geography, but rather see this as a call to attitudinal alignment, for at stake here is the posture of the engine room of our inner world toward the Lord. The word 'heart' here, *lēḇāḇ*, can of course point to our literal physical heart, but over and over again within the Hebrew Bible, it is referring to the core of a person's being, the inner workings of the mind and the centrality of the individual. Within the Scriptures we are urged to 'Keep your heart with all vigilance, for from it flow the springs of life' (Proverbs 4.23, ESV).

Solomon teaches us that our 'invironment' determines our environment, laying claim to a paradigm that the condition of our inner world is of more importance and consequence than the realities around us. Is it any wonder then that Solomon, as we have seen, asked for a 'listening heart' and when the Lord spoke through the Prophet Jeremiah, he longed for a people that would have his law written on their hearts and in whom he could create 'singleness of heart' or, read literally, 'one heart'?[6]

I've been a fan of Liverpool Football Club since 1974, and I've followed them through thick and thin, through the trophy-laden years and trophy-less years. I cheered them on when they became champions in 1990 and waited three decades to see them do the same in the 2019–2020 season. Anyone who knows me will testify that my passion for the Reds didn't wane during that long wait. However, if you didn't know me at all and had to discover which team I supported by the two biggest value indicators of my life, namely my time and my money, you would probably never guess which team I support. I rarely go to a game and, though I occasionally watch them on television, very little of my time and virtually none of my wealth goes to supporting the club. It is part of my world, but not central. Liverpool is my favourite team, but not the love of my life. It might be argued that I'm a fan, but not a supporter!

Loving the Lord with 'all our hearts' speaks of centrality, and in this context we are being called, in the light of hearing that 'the Lord our God the Lord is one, unique, unrivalled and alone', to place him at the centre of everything, thus allowing him to be the Lord of every facet of our lives. To love the Lord with 'all our hearts' is to position him at the centre of our relationships, finances, career and ambitions

---

6 1 Kings 3.9, Jeremiah 31.33 and 32.39.

and thus to refuse any area of our experience autonomy from his authority. Centrality means that whatever he wants, he can have and whatever he needs, we will give it.

From casual to intentional

'with *all your soul . . .* '

The Hebrew word here translated as soul is *nepeš*, and the first time it is seen within the Torah is Genesis 2.7 where we read: 'Then the LORD God formed a man from the dust of the ground and breathed into his nostrils the breath of life, and the man became a living being.'

The NIV translates it here as 'being' while other translations use 'soul', and the implication is that as God's breath of life entered the physical form of the man, he thus became a living being. In other words, according to the Genesis account, humans owe their being to God's breath.

A few years ago, my wife and I went to Rome for our wedding anniversary, and, like many others, we signed up for a tour around the Vatican. It was an experience I found both inspiring and disturbing. Our lovely Italian guide (who enjoyed addressing us as 'my darlings') became very excited as we were about to enter the Sistine Chapel. Before we went in, he gathered us into a huddle and in hushed tones spoke to us about Michelangelo's amazing work and, in particular, our guide's favourite piece, The Creation of Adam. If you're not familiar with the painting, Google it and you'll see how Michelangelo envisaged this creation moment. In it, God (complete with flowing grey hair and long grey beard) is reaching out his hand towards the man, who in turn is reaching out his hand to God. One of God's fingers is stretching to a finger that the man has extended, and the implication is that divine life passed to the man from God, from finger to finger. I discovered that day that Michelangelo was an amazing artist but a terrible theologian! Nothing could be further from

26

the truth, and how tragic a depiction of such a world-shaping moment. The first human was not created by a force from a finger but by breath from his face. This was not an impersonal power transaction, but something that was intended to be understood as personal, tender and intimate. As the man opened his eyes for the first time, the first thing he saw was the face of God! This was how the Lord made us, because this is how the Lord wants us!

In the light of hearing that 'the Lord our God the Lord is one, unique, unrivalled and alone', we are called to love him with 'all our souls' by giving back to him the life that he gave to us. To love him in this way is to surrender ourselves to him so that the life we have returns to the original purpose for which it was made. Paul picks up this very idea when writing to the believers in Rome: 'Therefore, I urge you, brothers and sisters, in view of God's mercy, to offer your bodies as a living sacrifice, holy and pleasing to God – this is your true and proper worship' (Romans 12.1). As Tim pointed out in the previous chapter, the progression is: 'In view of – offer – worship'.

Our greatest expression of worship is surrender. We do not surrender because we have to, but because we want to, and our surrender is not because we fear God, but because we love him. Voluntary, willing, generous surrender to the Lord is beautiful to him, having voluntarily, willingly and generously given life to us in the first place.

From good to best

'with *all your strength . . .* '

The word translated 'strength' is *me'ōḏ* and can literally mean very or muchness and points to force, energy, strength, might and enthusiasm. Perhaps, to summarize, we're being asked to love God with the very best of who we are and what we've got. This idea is represented beautifully in the Creation account, when we're told: 'God saw all that he had made, and it was very good' (Genesis 1.31).

27

God's good in this context was *me'ōḏ*: the best of himself given to creation in general and humanity specifically. In his giving his best, we get an insight into who he is, what he thinks of us and what he's prepared to do for us.

When it comes to Father's Day, I've tried not to place too much pressure on my children in terms of expecting special gifts. I've been happy with some chocolate and a nice card or, better still, everyone together for dinner. So when my youngest handed me a rather large present one year, I was both surprised and excited. I tore off the paper to discover a book of pictures, beautifully arranged and professionally designed, capturing some of our favourite moments together over the years. With the turning of each page, my emotions bubbled up until I could contain them no longer, and in front of everyone, I started to cry uncontrollably, which then made everyone else cry too. The gift was expensive financially (and she didn't have a lot of money) and in terms of creativity, time and effort. This was something she had planned for months, and even the selection of the pictures showed attention to detail and an insight into the joys at the core of our relationship. What I held was her best, and in that moment, I got an insight into who she was, what she thought of me and what she was prepared to do to please me.

In the light of hearing that 'the Lord our God the Lord is one, unique, unrivalled and alone', we are called to love him with 'all our strength' by giving him the best of ourselves in the very best way we can. Many have attempted to read a book like Leviticus and get confused over talk of sin, sacrifice and a lot of blood. But if we are prepared to dig into the heart of the book, *Vayikra*, which is Hebrew, can literally read 'and he called' – then we will see that this was about giving the best to a God who gave his best. Having given his best to us in creation and in salvation, he deserves our strength, the best of who we are and what we can offer. So many give what is left over and offer to him the dregs of what our day, creativity and energy have to offer, but the Shema calls us to give the best of all we are.

Soon after Moses gave these great words to God's people, they entered the land of promise and, off the back of conquest, settled into a new way of life. But before long, instead of looking to the one God, they looked to a king. Instead of remembering that the One lived among them and made them holy, places became sacred and replaced his glory. Eventually, rather than worshipping the One, they lusted after and gave themselves to other gods. Enter the prophets who proclaimed the voice of the Lord and became the conscience, of the Torah. Their messages, though varied and unique, echoed the same relentless ideas: 'Remember the One . . . return to the One . . . respond to the One!'

Jeremiah proclaimed: '"Return, faithless people," declares the Lord, "for I am your husband"' (Jeremiah 3.14).

Ezekiel lamented: 'You adulterous wife! You prefer strangers to your own husband' (Ezekiel 16.32).

Hosea pleaded: 'Return, O Israel to the Lord your God. Your sins have been your downfall' (Hosea 14.1).

It is no coincidence that one of the greatest 'return' moments in Israel's history was under a young king called Josiah, who discovered the Book of the Law, the book of Deuteronomy.[7] On *hearing* it read, he tore his clothes and led the nation to a place where they renewed their covenant with the One.[8]

Note how Josiah's legacy was remembered:

Neither before nor after Josiah was there a king like him who *turned* to the Lord as he did – with *all his heart* and with *all his soul* and with *all his strength*, in accordance with all the Law of Moses.'
(2 Kings 23.25, emphasis added)

---

7 Only Deuteronomy is referred to in the Torah as the Book of the Law, 28.61 and 29.21.

8 2 Kings 22.11 – the word translated 'hear' is *šāma'*.

The light and life of the Shema is unmissable in this text, and its shadow is undeniable in the life of Josiah and in the restoration of the nation. At the heart of its call was the revelation that the Lord is One, and with it, the only acceptable response to love him with the entirety of their being and behaviour.

The great prophet Jeremiah prophesied for around 41 years, witnessing the final and catastrophic demise of Judah and Jerusalem. His pain would have been all the greater, having started his ministry in the thirteenth year of Josiah's reign, and so he would have enjoyed the return of the people, which began in the eighteenth year of the young king's reign.[9] Perhaps this is why he relentlessly called the people to return over and over again, having seen the power of Shema at work in the life of the nation. Even in his darkest moment, as the reality of exile kicked in, with hope and faith he declared: 'Restore us to yourself, O Lord, that we may return; renew our days as of old' (Lamentations 5.21).

As the One, he is before all, above all and beyond all. As the One, he will not share his glory or his throne with another. As the One, he calls for and expects a response where heart, soul and strength are surrendered in their totality to him. As the One, he stands alone, unrivalled and apart, and therefore he and no one else deserves our worship.

We live in a world where so many ask the questions, 'Who am I and why am I here?' These may be useful questions to ask, but dangerously, *I* is at the centre of this enquiry, with life becoming a quest towards self-satisfaction and fulfilment. The Shema however, calls us to ask two deeper and much more significant questions, namely, 'Who is the Lord and what does he want?' Now he is at the centre, and our lives must then be interpreted in the light of his person, position and purpose. This tendency to place self at the centre can creep into our worship, our service and our ambitions and without

---

9   Jeremiah 1.2 and 2 Kings 22.3.

even realizing it, our behaviour can reflect more *me*ology than theology. When we put ourselves at the centre, God starts to look like us, shaped in our image and serving our desires; however, when he is at the centre, we start to look like him, moulded into his image and surrendered to his purpose.

The Shema reminds us that the Lord is One, unrivalled and alone, and that our only response to this revelation is to love him with our entire being, from which will flow an authentic lifestyle of worship.

Further resources for digging deeper

Dr John Andrews – *Extravagant – When Worship Becomes Lifestyle*
N. T. Wright – *For All God's Worth: True Worship and the Calling of the Church*
Matt Redman – *Facedown*
A. W. Tozer – *Worship: The Reason We Were Created – Collected Insights*

3

Who we worship – God the Son

DR HELEN MORRIS

Helen has been lecturing at Moorlands College for more than five years and is currently the acting director of Studies and lecturer in Applied Theology. Her doctoral studies were in the area of contemporary ecclesiology, which she completed at St Mary's University, Twickenham. Helen is in the worship band at her local church where she also preaches, and she is a ministry leader with Richmond holidays.

One of the verses that often comes up when talking about worship is Romans 12.1, as you will see throughout this book. Tim and John have both mentioned it already. It says, 'Therefore, I urge you, brothers and sisters, in view of God's mercy, to offer your bodies as a living sacrifice, holy and pleasing to God – this is your true and proper worship.'[1] Paul, the author of Romans, exhorts his readers to give their whole lives in worship to God. Central to this 'true and proper worship' is the transformation of the believer's mind so that they grasp God's character and purposes better. Such revelation leads to a humble perspective on one's own life and a magnified view of the grandeur and majesty of God (Romans 12.2–3). Paul uses the word 'God' to refer to God the Father[2]; however, Paul makes clear elsewhere in his writings that the 'who' to whom whole-life worship is due is the triune God, who is

---

1   All the Bible quotations in this chapter are from the NIV 2011 translation.

2   e.g. Romans 6:23; 7:25; 8:3

three persons in one.[3] God is to be worshipped as Father, Son and Spirit. To help us grow in our worship of the Son, Jesus, I'm going to explore Hebrews, which contains beautiful and powerful reflections on the nature and work of Jesus. As we reflect on who Jesus is and what he has done for us, I pray that our attitude before God will increasingly be one of humility and awe and that we will be inspired towards the whole-life worship that Paul urges us to.

The Sovereign King

We believe in one God,
the Father, the Almighty,
maker of heaven and earth,
of all that is, seen and unseen.
We believe in one Lord, Jesus Christ,
the only Son of God,
eternally begotten of the Father,
God from God, Light from Light,
true God from true God,
begotten, not made,
of one Being with the Father.
Through him all things were made.
For us and for our salvation
he came down from heaven:
by the power of the Holy Spirit
he became incarnate from the Virgin Mary,
and was made man.[4]

3   For a detailed assessment of Paul's trinitarian theology, I recommend Wesley Hill, *Paul and the Trinity: Persons, Relations and the Pauline Letters* (Grand Rapids: Eerdmans, 2015).

4   The Nicene Creed (taken from <http://www.anglicansonline.org/basics/nicene .html>).

> The Son is the radiance of God's glory and the exact representation of his being, sustaining all things by his powerful word. (Hebrews 1.3)

The author of Hebrews emphasizes the humanity of Jesus. Because Jesus is fully human, the author assures us, he can be both the perfect high priest and suffering servant. The early believers included Jesus in their worship; however, because they recognized that, alongside being fully human, Jesus is fully God. This central doctrine of the Christian faith, Jesus's full humanity and full divinity, is awe-inspiring. The well-known proverb asserts that familiarity breeds contempt. Perhaps more often it breeds complacency. Whenever I dwell on the truth of Jesus's divine and human nature long enough for its mind-blowing immensity to seep through my settled familiarity, I am awestruck afresh. Christmas is a time when my appreciation of this truth is renewed once more. Lines such as, 'See within a manger lies, he who built the starry skies'[5] express with simplicity, and yet profundity, why Jesus is worthy to receive 'praise and honour and glory and power, for ever and ever!' (Revelation 5.13) It is noteworthy, therefore, that the author's emphasis on Jesus's humanity is preceded with a celebration of Jesus's divinity.

Expressing mind-blowing beliefs pushes the limits of human articulation: how do we describe and explain truths that are beyond full human comprehension? One of the best ways is through comparison. For example, while I sat through many physics lectures having no clue what my lecturer was talking about, studying sports science and physics at university left me with an interest in popular-level physics, even if I could never get my head around the equations that undergird it. I am particularly fascinated by the very big and the very small. When trying to understand the ginormous and the tiny, comparison is more impactful than numbers. If, for instance, I told

----

5   From the carol 'See Amid the Winter's Snow'.

you that the average neutron star[6] has a density of 10^{14} g/cc, unless you work with such numbers, this might be meaningless to you. If, however, I tell you that a teaspoon of neutron star contains the mass of 200 million elephants (or all the people on earth), we have a fuller appreciation of how dense these stars are.

The author of Hebrews adopts a similar tactic. He expresses Jesus's greatness through comparison with people and entities that were particularly impressive to his first readers: angels, the earth, Moses, the high priest, Melchizedek, the temple, sacrifices and the covenant.[7] These comparisons may not be as impactful for us as they were to the first readers of Hebrews. For instance, in the Western church, we tend not to think that much about angels except at Christmas time, when we're reminded of their significance through the account of Jesus's birth. In contrast, angels are very significant in Judaism and early Christianity. The Old Testament presents God as the unopposed king of creation, surrounded by a great entourage of angelic servants. These servants honour God in worship and carry out his will by such acts as delivering his messages, protecting his servants, fighting his enemies, and bringing about his judgement. In addition, between the end of the Old Testament and the beginning of the New Testament, angels were increasingly presented as mediators between human beings and God. Therefore, alongside emphasizing Jesus's supremacy over angels in terms of glory and honour, the author of Hebrews also points out that if you think a faithful servant is a good mediator between the king and his subjects, how much better is the king's son![8]

---

6   A neutron star is what forms when a star burns up its energy and starts to collapse in on itself.

7   The technical term for such comparisons is *synkrisis*. The aim of this type of rhetoric is to emphasize and affirm the honour of the one being praised by comparing their nature and achievements with other honourable figures. For more information on this, see David A. deSilva, *Perseverance in Gratitude: A Socio-Rhetorical Commentary on the Epistle "to the Hebrews"* (Grand Rapids: Eerdmans, 2000), 93.

8   deSilva, *Perseverance in Gratitude*, 93–94.

A key role credited to Jesus in the New Testament is that, as the king's son, he establishes God's kingdom. The author of Hebrews highlights this point through quoting various Old Testament texts. The New Testament authors' use of the Old Testament is a really interesting area to explore.[9] The common thread is that all these authors read the Old Testament in light of their knowledge and experience of Jesus. For example, David deSilva argues that, for Hebrews's author, the various parts of the Old Testament are like 'small and scattered pieces of a great jigsaw puzzle, which all come together when seen in light of the final revelation in the Son. The person and work of Jesus is the complete picture.'[10]

Psalm 2 is one of the key jigsaw pieces referred to by New Testament authors. In Hebrews, the author quotes from this Psalm to highlight Jesus's establishment of God's kingdom, 'You are my Son; today I have become your Father' (Hebrews 1.5 cf. Psalm 2.7). Through this quotation, Hebrews's author affirms Jesus's relationship with God as his father and reveals Jesus as God's anointed king who rules the earth and defeats God's enemies (Psalm 2.1–12). To emphasize this point even further, the author of Hebrews also quotes from Psalm 45.6–7, 'But about the Son he says, "Your throne, O God, will last for ever and ever; a sceptre of justice will be the sceptre of your kingdom"' (Hebrews 1.8). This prompts the questions: in what way does Jesus bring about God's kingdom and what is the nature of this kingdom and Jesus's reign? To these questions we'll now turn.

The Servant King

For our sake he was crucified under Pontius Pilate;
he suffered death and was buried.

---

9   If you want to read more on this area, I'd recommend Richard B. Hays, *Echoes of Scripture in the Letters of Paul* and *Reading Backwards: Figural Christology and the Fourfold Gospel Witness* (Waco: Baylor University Press, 2014).

10 deSilva, *Perseverance in Gratitude*, 86.

On the third day he rose again
in accordance with the Scriptures;
he ascended into heaven
and is seated at the right hand of the Father.
He will come again in glory to judge the living and the dead,
and his kingdom will have no end.[11]

Since the children have flesh and blood, he too shared in their humanity so that by his death he might break the power of him who holds the power of death – that is, the devil – and free those who all their lives were held in slavery by their fear of death. (Hebrews 2.14–15)

At Moorlands College, where I work as a lecturer in Applied Theology, in one of their first assignments, the students are asked to articulate the gospel in three minutes to a particular context. We introduced this task because, although the gospel is foundational to the Christian faith, it is not easy to express succinctly what the gospel is. Presenting the gospel in a short period of time is particularly challenging when, as modelled by the New Testament church, we try to use concepts that are meaningful to those listening and avoid Christian jargon. One way that the gospel has been expressed succinctly is through the bridge diagram. In this diagram, an individual stands on one side of an uncrossable chasm and God on the other. The chasm is caused by sin, which creates a barrier between humans and God, resulting in eternal death. The cross fills this chasm, acting as a bridge between people and God, enabling a person who puts their trust in Jesus to be reconciled with God and receive the gift of eternal life.[12] This type of gospel presentation has led many people to faith,

---

11 The Nicene Creed.

12 See, for example, the Navigators 'Bridge to Life' webpage (<https://www.navigators.org/resource/the-bridge-to-life>).

which is a cause for much thanksgiving. It conveys simply and effectively a core truth of the gospel that Jesus's death on the cross enables people to be forgiven and reconciled; with God. It is easy to remember and communicate, which gives people the confidence to share their faith with others. However, despite these great strengths, there are some weaknesses to this type of presentation.[13] These weaknesses are best seen by comparing the bridge-diagram presentation with what Scot McKnight refers to as the 'apostolic gospel tradition' conveyed in 1 Corinthians 15.[14]

> Now, brothers and sisters, I want to remind you of the gospel I preached to you, which you received and on which you have taken your stand. By this gospel you are saved, if you hold firmly to the word I preached to you. Otherwise, you have believed in vain. For what I received I passed on to you as of first importance: that Christ died for our sins according to the Scriptures, that he was buried, that he was raised on the third day according to the Scriptures and that he appeared to Cephas, and then to the Twelve. (1 Corinthians 15.1–5)

Wherever there is repetition in the Bible, the words repeated are particularly important. Did you notice the repetition in these verses?

> For what I received I passed on to you as of first importance: that Christ died for our sins *according to the Scriptures*, that

---

13 See Pete Ward, *Liquid Ecclesiology: The Gospel and the Church* (Leiden: Brill, 2017), esp. Part II. For a fuller outline of Ward's arguments and my response to them, you can read my chapter in a forthcoming book called *Evangelicals Engaging with Practical Theology: Theology that Impacts the Church and the World,* published by Routledge, edited by myself and Helen Cameron and due for publication in 2021. The chapter is called "A wonderful plan for my life? Pete Ward's 'the Gospel and Change' in dialogue with Charles Taylor."

14 Scot McKnight, *The King Jesus Gospel: The Original Good News Revisited* (Grand Rapids: Brazos Press, 2014), esp. Chapter 4.

he was buried, that he was raised on the third day *according to the Scriptures*

In a right desire to communicate the gospel fully to people, we can be tempted to imply that what we say in two or three minutes is all that need be said. In contrast, Paul's summary emphasizes to his hearers that there is more to understand and learn. While the core of the gospel is focused on Jesus's death and resurrection, Paul's repetition of 'according to the Scriptures' indicates that understanding the significance of these acts requires a continuing process of digging deeper into the story of Scripture. The author of Hebrews concurs with Paul's emphasis. In fact, there are so many references to the Old Testament that scholars often assume that Hebrews was written primarily to Jewish believers. However, somewhat pointedly, David deSilva contends that this argument is based on the wrong assumption that the first Gentile believers had as little knowledge of the Old Testament as many Christians have today![15] In contrast, passages such as 1 Corinthians 10.1–13 (the Corinthian church consisted mainly of Gentile believers) demonstrate that Gentile believers were expected to learn the Old Testament and seek to understand who Jesus is and what he has done in reference to it.

Two Old Testament themes that the author of Hebrews draws on are atonement and sacrifice.

For this reason he had to be made like them, fully human in every way, in order that he might become a merciful and faithful high priest in service to God, and that he might make atonement for the sins of the people. (Hebrews 2.17)

Just as people are destined to die once, and after that to face judgement, so Christ was sacrificed once to take away the sins of many; and he will appear a second time, not to bear

15 See deSilva, *Perseverance in Gratitude*, 4.

sin, but to bring salvation to those who are waiting for him. (Hebrews 9.27–28)

You're probably familiar with the word 'scapegoat' – referring to a person who takes the blame for someone else's wrongdoing. The phrase originates from Leviticus 16 and its description of the Day of Atonement. The Day of Atonement took place once a year and, on that day, the high priest offered a bull as a sacrifice for his and his family's sin and then took two goats. One of the goats was sacrificed as a sin offering for the people's wrongdoing. The high priest then confessed the people's sins while laying his hands on the other goat's head. This goat was sent away into the wilderness to symbolize the people's sins being taken away. Only on this day, once a year, could the high priest enter the Most Holy Place, which was the part of the tabernacle (or temple) where God's presence dwelt most fully.

By ascribing the role of atonement to Jesus, the author of Hebrews conveys the amazing truth that, through his death, Jesus is the ultimate sacrifice and scapegoat. The notion of a human fulfilling this role is pre-empted in the Old Testament through the image of the Suffering Servant. Isaiah 52.13–53.12 is the longest Suffering Servant passage and is alluded to by the author of Hebrews in the language of *taking away* and *bearing* sin:

> Surely he took up our pain
>   and bore our suffering,
>   yet we considered him punished by God,
>   stricken by him, and afflicted.
> But he was pierced for our transgressions,
>   he was crushed for our iniquities;
>   the punishment that brought us peace
>   was on him,
>   and by his wounds we are healed.
>   (Isaiah 53.4–5)

Importantly, though, this Suffering Servant passage doesn't end with the Servant's suffering but with his vindication and victory:

> After he has suffered,
>> he will see the light of life and be satisfied;
>> by his knowledge my righteous servant will justify
>>> many,
>> and he will bear their iniquities.
> Therefore I will give him a portion among the great,
>> and he will divide the spoils with the strong,
>> because he poured out his life unto death,
>> and was numbered with the transgressors.
>> For he bore the sin of many,
>>> and made intercession for the transgressors.
> (Isaiah 53.11–12)

The Servant's vindication and victory in Isaiah 53 prefigures a key theme in the New Testament authors' presentation of Jesus (one that isn't present in the bridge-diagram). This is the inseparable connection between Jesus's crucifixion and kingship. The author of Hebrews highlights this connection when he notes in 1.3, 'After he had provided purification for sins, he sat down at the right hand of the Majesty in heaven.' The description of Jesus sitting at God's right hand brings to mind Revelation 5, where the connection between Jesus's death and dominion is powerfully portrayed through the image of Jesus, the slain lamb, as the triumphant lion of Judah who establishes God's kingdom on earth. Paul's presentation of the gospel in 1 Corinthians 15 conveys the same connection. Read through the whole chapter and see how Paul moves from Jesus's death and resurrection to the hope of Jesus's future return and accompanying establishment of God's kingdom.

Why is Jesus's death so intricately connected to his enthronement? Hebrews answers this question in the verse I quoted at the start of this section, 'he too shared in their humanity so that by his death he might break the power of him who holds the power of death – that is, the devil – and free those who all their lives were held in slavery by their fear of death' (Hebrews 2.14–15). From the moment the serpent appears in the Garden of Eden to lure Adam and Eve away from trust in God, a war is unleashed. It's not a war between two sides of near equal strength, wrestling it out until one gets the upper hand. Rather, it is a battle between the all-powerful sovereign creator of the universe and a vastly inferior enemy who has just two main weapons: accusation and deceit. So long as humanity, through the devil's temptation and human rebellion, are drawn away from faith in God's perfect love and thereby face his judgement, people remain alienated from God, experiencing the injustice, oppression and slavery that result from rejecting his goodness – abandoning the spring of living water and building broken cisterns of their own (Jeremiah 2.13). By making atonement through his crucifixion and resurrection, Jesus breaks the power of sin, silencing the devil's accusations. By revealing God to us, Jesus overcomes the devil's deceit. Through his ascension to heaven, Jesus empowers the church by his Spirit to expand God's kingdom on earth. Jesus's return brings the full establishment of God's kingdom when all that stands against God's character and purposes is fully defeated and God's people enter their 'Sabbath-rest' (Hebrews 4).

Jesus is the servant king.[16] Meditating on Jesus's sacrifice stirs our hearts to worship. For the New Testament authors, such worship is to be expressed in words of praise and thanksgiving. It is also to be expressed in following Jesus's example, demonstrating a willingness to suffer when our service of Jesus leads to hardship.

Serving the King

We believe in the Holy Spirit, the Lord, the giver of life,
who proceeds from the Father and the Son.

---

16 As celebrated in the 1980s Graham Kendrick song of this title.

With the Father and the Son he is worshiped and glorified.
He has spoken through the Prophets.
We believe in one holy catholic and apostolic Church.
We acknowledge one baptism for the forgiveness of sins.
We look for the resurrection of the dead,
and the life of the world to come.[17]

One of the subjects I teach at Moorlands College is the book of Revelation. In Revelation, there is often a contrast between what John hears and what he sees. Revelation 5, which I referred to above, is a great example of this. In 5.5, John hears words saying, 'Do not weep! See, the Lion of the tribe of Judah, the Root of David, has triumphed.' He then sees 'a Lamb, looking as if it had been slain'. In Revelation 6, John hears the number of those sealed, 144,000 (6.4), and then sees 'a great multitude that no one could count, from every nation, tribe, people and language' (6.9). In both instances, what is seen sheds light on what is heard and vice versa. So in Revelation 5, the contrast between the images of the lion and the lamb show that what might look like defeat (the suffering and death of the lamb) is actually a powerful and decisive victory. In Revelation 6, if we do a bit of maths, we see that 144,000 is 12x12x1000. Numbers are used symbolically in Revelation. Twelve is the number of God's people (the twelve tribes of Israel and twelve disciples). Squaring it indicates completeness. A thousand symbolizes a vast number. Therefore, 144,000 is symbolic of the completeness and vastness of God's people, which John's vision reveals to consist of a countless multitude from the four corners of the earth.[18] In Revelation 21, there is another contrast between what John hears and sees. He hears in 21.9, 'Come, I will show you

---

17 The Nicene Creed.

18 For further information on numbers in Revelation, see Ian Paul, *Revelation: An Introduction and Commentary* (Nottingham: IVP, 2018), 34–39. For an even more in-depth analysis, see Richard Bauckham, *The Climax of Prophecy: Studies on the Book of Revelation* (Edinburgh: T. & T. Clark, 1993), 29-37.

the bride, the wife of the Lamb.' However, what he then sees is not a woman dressed in wedding clothes, but a massive gold cube![19] What is going on?

Let's go back a moment to the point I made earlier about comparisons helping us grasp mind-blowing facts. Another way that we can be helped with this is through models. Perhaps you can remember as a child making a model of the solar system? You made a metre-wide Sun, then a 1cm-wide Earth and placed it 100 metres away from the Sun. You then made a 2cm-wide Pluto and walked 4km before putting it down. Well, I suspect you didn't go quite as to scale as this – more likely, you just put different types of seed at various points in a school hallway! The point is that, like comparisons, models can bring home the vastness of the universe more powerfully than numbers. As well as helping us understand the vastness of the universe, models can help us grasp truths about God. In Hebrews, for example, the tabernacle and temple are described as a model of heaven (Hebrews 8.5). Within Israelite worship, these were the places where God's presence was thought to dwell most fully, with his presence experienced in its greatest intensity in the Most Holy Place.[20] As I noted earlier in this chapter, because human sin alienates people from God, the Most Holy Place could only be entered once a year by the high priest, and sacrifice was the God-given gift that enabled this access. For the author of Hebrews, Jesus is the perfect high priest and the perfect sacrifice who opens up not just the model of heaven but heaven itself. In addition, the sacrifice Jesus offers doesn't need to be repeated year on year, but was once and for all (Hebrews 8 and 9).

Seeing the Most Holy Place as a model of heaven helps us to understand why, when John is told to look at the bride of Christ, he sees

---

19 John writes, 'The city was laid out like a square, as long as it was wide . . . The wall was made of jasper, and the city of pure gold, as pure as glass' (Revelation 21.16–18).

20 G. K. Beale, *The Temple and the Church's Mission: A Biblical Theology of the Dwelling Place of God* (Downers Grove: IVP, 2004), 31–56.

a giant gold cube. In the temple and tabernacle, the Most Holy Place was cubic in shape. 'The bride' is 'the Holy City' (21.2), and John's vision reveals that this city is the true Most Holy Place (21.10–21). Whereas in Old Testament worship, the location of God's most intimate presence used to be accessible by one man once a year, in the new creation, all of God's people have access to the fullness of God's presence continually and permanently. John's vision of the new creation, where God's presence is experienced fully by his people, is a hope for the future. However, it is also something that the Church experiences, in part, now. In Ephesians 5.21–33, for example, the metaphor of the Church as Christ's bride is applied to the Church in the present. This metaphor speaks of the intimacy of the relationship between Christ and his Church (see especially 5.32). In Ephesians 2.11–22, Paul describes the Church as a temple of God's Spirit. These metaphors of the Church as Christ's bride and a temple of his Spirit should spur us to thanksgiving and action. God's greatest gift is the gift of himself.[21] Therefore, recognizing that the Church is where God dwells most intimately with his people inspires us to praise.

Seeing the Church as God's dwelling place should also inspire believers to help one another encounter him. 'Let us not us not give up meeting together', the author of Hebrews enjoins us (10.25). Moreover, taking hold of our identity as Christ's bride and a temple of God's Spirit motivates us to confess and put aside those areas of selfishness, impurity and darkness that are so out of place in the light of God's presence. The metaphors of bride and temple also shed light on the Church's calling. As the place where God's presence now dwells most fully, the Church is called to demonstrate and bear witness to how things will be when the whole of creation is filled with God's glory and presence. Before Jesus returns, the Church will do this imperfectly – we know we're works in progress! In the midst of its

---

21 John Piper, *God is the Gospel* (Wheaton: Crossway, 2005), esp. Chapter 3.

imperfection, though, the Church is called to demonstrate the hope of heaven as well as communicate this hope.[22] Bishop Graham Cray expresses this calling well when he writes,

> If there is to be no poverty in the new heavens and earth, the Church should be seen as a community that cares for the poor. If there is to be no injustice, it is to be seen as a community that challenges injustice. If we will see Christ face to face, then the Church becomes the place where we learn to believe without having seen. If we will enjoy the gracious hospitality of God, the Church must be a place of welcome and hospitality.[23]

For the author of Hebrews, the celebration of Jesus and the hope that's found in him should lead believers to demonstrate God's grace and goodness in their thoughts, actions and words. As we reflect on who Jesus is and what he has done for us, may we also be stirred to respond in these ways.

Persevere in gratitude

As I write, America is drawing near to its next election. Around election time, well-known politicians and celebrities speak or tweet in praise of their favoured candidate. However, their aim is not just to praise the candidate, they also hope to provoke their hearers into action – they want them to vote for the person they're rooting for! In Hebrews, the author expresses his praise to Jesus by presenting the

---

22 Alongside the hope found in Jesus, the Church needs to be prepared to communicate the warning of judgement for those who don't accept the grace given through Christ. The author of Hebrews does not pull his punches in this regard (see, for example, Hebrews 10.26–31).

23 Graham Cray, "Communities of the Kingdom," in *Fresh Expressions of Church and the Kingdom of God*, eds. Graham Cray, Aaron Kennedy and Ian Mobsby (Norwich: Canterbury Press, 2021), 18.

amazing truths about who Jesus is and what he has done with beauty and intricacy. However, like the politician who speaks, in favour of the presidential candidate, the author of Hebrews also intends that his praise of Jesus will stir his readers to action.

In particular, the author intends that his celebration of Jesus will inspire his readers to stand firm in their commitment to Christ. Some are tempted to turn back.[24] They have faced difficulties because of their faith in Jesus and are wondering if life would be easier and better if they reintegrated into wider culture.[25] The author of Hebrews acknowledges the difficulties that his readers are facing but finds it astonishing that some are thinking of abandoning their faith. To encourage his readers to stand firm, he urges them to look to the future and the hope of salvation that awaits Christ's return (10.36). He warns of judgement for those who spurn God's gift of grace (10.31), and he enjoins his readers to fix their eyes on Jesus, put off those sins that entangle and not lose heart (12.1–3). He exhorts them to live at peace with each other and love one another as brothers and sisters in Christ (12.14 and 13.1). He implores them to stay committed to the truth of the gospel and not be led astray by strange teachings (13.9–14). He urges them to *perseverance in gratitude*, as David deSilva brilliantly entitles his commentary.

Perhaps we can relate to the struggles that the author of Hebrews is addressing. We, too, can be tempted to turn aside from devotion to Christ when our commitment to him means that we are looked down on, ostracized or even attacked. I hope that celebrating Jesus will inspire us to stand firm in our devotion to him. I pray that we will persevere in gratitude as we reflect on who Jesus is and all he has done for us.

---

24 (2.1–3; 3.7–19; 5.11–6.12; 10.19–39).

25 On the difficulties that the first readers of Hebrews were facing, see deSilva, *Perseverence in Gratitude*, 11.

Further resources for digging deeper

To dig deeper into the book of Hebrews, I recommend David deSilva's Hebrews commentary, *Perseverance in Gratitude: A Socio-Rhetorical Commentary on the Epistle "to the Hebrews"*.

For a biblical overview of worship, see Daniel I. Block, *For the Glory of God, Recovering a Biblical Theology of Worship*.

To read more about the significance of Jesus's death, I recommend:

John Stott – *The Cross of Christ*.

Fleming Rutledge – *The Crucifixion: Understanding the Death of Jesus Christ*.

4

The Holy Spirit in worship

DR NICK DRAKE

Nick is associate vicar at Gas Street in Birmingham. Having been a worship leader for many years and worship pastor at St Paul's Hammersmith, Nick studied at King's College London before completing his doctoral research into Pentecostal-Charismatic Worship at the University of Birmingham. Together with his wife, Becky, Nick co-founded Worship For Everyone, a multi-generational worship movement and teaches at Worship Central as well as St Mellitus College.

Have you ever mimed in church? Basically faked the fact you're singing? As a teenager, I did it all the time. I hated singing in church but felt the social pressure to conform and so would mime the words. I looked like I was engaged and part of the worshipping community, but I wasn't actually present. This singing together thing was *not* for me.

That all changed when I encountered the Holy Spirit. I was filled with the life of the Spirit, and suddenly I couldn't *stop* singing! The Spirit had brought me freedom (2 Corinthians 3.17). In fact, my whole life since that point has been about leading people closer to Jesus in sung worship! It began to make sense that in Ephesians 5.18–20, Paul seems to be saying that there is a link between getting filled with the Holy Spirit and singing – wanting to praise God, opening our hearts with everything we have to say thank you and to tell him he's amazing and unrivalled. He writes:

49

> Be filled with the Spirit, speaking to one another with psalms, hymns, and songs from the Spirit. Sing and make music from your heart to the Lord, always giving thanks to God the Father for everything, in the name of our Lord Jesus Christ.

What I had experienced working upon me and within me was God's relational presence – the activity of the Holy Spirit empowering me to worship my Maker. This is the key role the Spirit plays in our times of worship. He is working upon us and within us to release our hearts to praise the one worthy of all praise – Jesus – and to enjoy intimate relationship with our Heavenly Father. It is the Holy Spirit who empowers our worship, so in this chapter we're going to look at some of the amazing things he does and how he does it.

Glorifying Jesus and experiencing his resurrection life

The Holy Spirit's person and work is an essential feature of true Christian worship;[1] it's not just something Pentecostals or Charismatics have added on in the last hundred years! One of the earliest theologians of the church, St Basil the Great, said: 'For it is impossible to worship the Son, save by the Holy Spirit; impossible to call upon the Father, save by the Spirit of adoption.'[2] In fact, there are two key words that express our relationship to God and declare praise that the Bible says we can't even say (or sing!) without the power of the Spirit in us. The first we're going to explore is 'Jesus is Lord' (Kyrios) (1 Corinthians 12.3).[3]

---

1 Philippians 3.3 says it is *by* the Spirit that we worship.

2 P. Schaff and H. Wace (Eds.), B. Jackson (Trans.), *St. Basil: Letters and Select Works* (Vol. 8, p. 18). New York: Christian Literature Company.

3 'No one can say "Jesus is Lord", except by the Holy Spirit.'

Declaring Jesus is Lord is the core lyric to our worship. It stands in the line of the Old Testament core lyric 'YHWH Reigns!'[4] and is a multi-faceted expression of our surrender and allegiance, combined with his unrivalled power and centrality to all existence. Jesus himself tells us that the Spirit will always glorify the Son (John 16.14), and here is one of the most powerful but simple truths of what the Spirit does when we worship: he directs our attention and focus and provokes our mouths to open and declare afresh 'Jesus is Lord!' Jesus reigns and rules, and everything is under his feet! This dynamic work of the Spirit is perhaps what the Psalmist knew when he prayed 'O Lord open my lips and my mouth will declare your praise!' (Psalm 51.15). The Spirit works to lead our worship to be Jesus-centered and to unite us in declaring in praise his priority in our lives over all other claims of authority or allegiance.

Not only does the Spirit enable our praise of Jesus and direct our hearts to his supremacy won through the cross, but he also acts to connect us directly and experientially to this reality. This is where it gets really wild. The Apostle Paul writes, 'For if we have been united with him in a death like his, we will certainly also be united with him in a resurrection like his' (Romans 6.5). How are we 'united to him'? How do we encounter in a powerful and intimate way the life of God in Christ *for us*? His resurrection life? *By the power and activity of the Holy Spirit.* The great Reformer John Calvin put it starkly: 'as long as Christ remains outside of us, and we are separated from him, all that he has suffered and done for the salvation of the human race remains useless and of no value for us.'[5]

---

4 'The Lord reigns' or 'the Lord is King' is recognized as a central declaration of the 'songbook of the temple' – the Psalms. For example, the opening line of Psalm 93 says: 'The Lord reigns, he is robed in majesty; the Lord is robed in majesty and armed with strength.'

5 John Calvin, Institutes of the Christian Religion, 1559, trans. Ford Lewis Battles, 2 vols. (London; printed in U.S.A.: S.C.M. Press, 1961). 3.1.1.

Perhaps one way to understand what the Spirit does in worship is to imagine yourself at a museum. This isn't a perfect analogy, but it may help you grasp what we're getting at here. You've gone to view a rare historic artefact. You've read a lot of background information about the artefact, and you can't wait to encounter it up close and for real, but when you get to the museum, you're dismayed to see the artefact is kept on a pedestal behind a Perspex box. You may be technically in the same room as the artefact, but you leave feeling like you didn't truly encounter it. You weren't close enough.

The Holy Spirit works in our worship, to connect us, or *relate* us to the living reality of the risen Jesus. All that is in Jesus (his worldview, his heart, his resurrection life) are activated or made real in our lives by the Holy Spirit as we worship. The Holy Spirit makes what many see as history (the Bible stories of Jesus) reality – Christ in us, the hope of glory! It's the moment when head knowledge drops to heart knowledge; intellectual theory becomes life experience; stories of old become present today. He joins our lives to the life of the risen Jesus as we worship, as he leads us in declaring 'Jesus is Lord' right now, in our lives!

This experiential reality in which the Holy Spirit facilitates our participation and brings himself is what the Dominican theologian Jean Corbon calls the deep 'fountain' of worship[6] and what is sometimes talked of in contemporary church as 'the presence of God' in worship. No matter what the outward forms of worship are that we prefer or in which we regularly participate (liturgical, sung, sacramental), the deeper fountain remains the same and available to all. The 'all-embracing event of Christ'[7] is enterable, like walking through the back of the Narnia wardrobe, by the person and work of the Holy Spirit as we worship. He makes real in our world,

---

6   Jean Corbon, *The Wellspring of Worship*, Ignatius Press, San Francisco 2005, 24.

7   Corbon, *Wellspring*, 25.

in our worship, the work of the Father with and through the Son right now, today![8]

This is why an understanding of the Holy Spirit, seen in a Trinitarian context, is so crucial for beholding the wonder of what happens in the deepest sense when Christians worship. We start seeing why the early Church used the word *perichoresis* to describe the Trinity. This is a theological concept which means the Trinity rotates around and makes space for one another, which some visualize as a dance. The Spirit truly does place us right in the middle of 'God's Great Dance Floor', as a recent worship song put it! Participation in the life of God is the number one outworking of Spirit-led worship. As I hope you're seeing by now, *all* (true) Christian worship is 'Spirit-led'.

This is why a prayerful dependency on him is so key to authentic and powerful worship. We can't make the presence of God come,[9] but we can posture ourselves and invite him to work deeply within us as we worship. This is what is meant when people pray 'Come Holy Spirit' in worship, but it also can be prayed in private before meeting together. I have made it my own personal discipline to always pray before I do anything, 'Come Holy Spirit; I need you Holy Spirit. Come and fill me and work through me in your power. Amen.' It acts as a crucial reminder that in and of myself I am not enough for what God can do in this moment. It invites a synergy – my work, submitted to, dependent on and working with God's work. The Greek Orthodox thinker Nikos Nissiotis invites us to see the Church as existing in a perpetual state of invitation to the Spirit to 'come'

---

8   It can be seen by what we have been talking about already that what is meant by that is not merely an 'omni-presence' – the always with us, abiding presence that is the very nature of what it means to be God – but a 'manifest' presence. This 'manifest' presence of God in worship is his movement towards, amid and within the congregation as we gather to worship and open our hearts and lives afresh to him.

9   'A human self-making of divine presence is a contradiction in terms and a thoroughly futile endeavour.' A. Loades, *Finding New Sense in the 'Sacramental'*, in G.Rowell & C.Hall (eds.), The Gestures of God, London: Continuum, 2004, p. 162.

('epiclesis').[10] This is where the church at worship is powerful; this is how we each need to take responsibility to come to worship in prayerful openness and hunger for the Spirit.

Powerful witness

This work and activity of the Holy Spirit, joining us to the reality of Christ in worship, is why sung worship can be so powerful in evangelism. I remember when I was leading my first Alpha group, we had one guest who turned up week after week, soaking up all the information about Jesus, but he just couldn't and wouldn't move to a place of personal belief and wanting to follow Jesus. Then one week, in the time of sung worship, I looked around and saw he had tears streaming down his face. Several weeks later, we baptized him and he went on to get married to a wonderful Christian woman. In that time of worship, the Holy Spirit had taken everything he had learnt about Jesus and dropped it from his head to his heart. The 'Perspex box' had been lifted.

Spiritually alive worship, that makes visible and invitational the reality declared by 'Jesus is Lord', is crucial for the Church to be a powerful witness in its worship. The Church at worship is meant to be a fantastic divine-human event! John Colwell rightly challenges us: '[people] may expect to receive a welcome, the warmth of friendship . . . children's work and youth work, comfortable seating, engaging preaching – but even the most theologically unaware and undiscerning expect something more profound from or through a church: they expect to be encountered by God.'[11] So when we worship, let's come expectant, standing on the foundation of the word of God, ready to 'lean in' and give everything we've got to the one who has given everything for us.

---

10 Nikos A Nissiotis, 'Worship, Eucharist, and "Intercommunion": An Orthodox Reflection', *Studia Liturgica* 2 (1963).

11 John Colwell, *Promise and Presence*, Milton Keynes: Paternoster, 2005, p. 257.

Enjoying the Father and experiencing our new identity

We have explored how the Spirit enables our response to God as we declare 'Jesus is Lord'. The second word that we can only say or sing by the work of the Holy Spirit is 'Abba' – Father. Paul writes in Romans 8.14–16:

> For those who are led by the Spirit of God are the children of God. The Spirit you received does not make you slaves, so that you live in fear again; rather, the Spirit you received brought about your adoption to sonship. And by him we cry, 'Abba, Father.' The Spirit himself testifies with our spirit that we are God's children.

What clues does this give us to what the Spirit does in worship?

In the press recently there was a story of a five-year-old boy called Michael who invited his whole kindergarten class to the courtroom in Michigan to witness his legal adoption to his new parents. There was a fantastic photograph of Michael seated with his new family, with all his classmates and teacher from kindergarten in the background, waving red hearts they had cut out to bring along.[12] Michael had been welcomed into his new family in an atmosphere of celebration. He had received a whole new identity, and, in that moment, it was publicly, visibly, signed and sealed.

Adoption is the image used by Paul when he expresses the overarching story of what God has done for us through his son Jesus. We have become sons and daughters of God, brothers and sisters of Jesus (Hebrews 2), part of the big family of God. This is the place of

---

12 <https://www.bbc.co.uk/news/world-us-canada-50683948>

healing, restoration and flourishing. This is the place of safety, from which true, unconditional, cross-shaped love can heal us.

In worship, so much work is done by the Spirit in this realm of our identity. There is a shift going on in each of us from old creation to new, out of darkness into a 'marvellous light'.[13] We are no longer 'in Adam' but 'in Christ' – how? By the power of the Spirit at work as we open our hearts, our mouths and our lives to God in praise and surrender. The Spirit in worship acts to fulfil Paul's prayer that we might be 'rooted, and established in love' (Ephesians 3.17). As we pour out our praises, declaring Jesus is Lord and honouring our Father in Heaven as our true source and Creator, so the Spirit pours out into our hearts the 'family' love (Romans 5.5). Worship is a discipline that helps us grasp with every fibre of our being how 'wide and long and high and deep is the love of Christ' (Ephesians 3.18).

When we worship, we are therefore a family coming together to celebrate what God has done in Christ and to welcome and encourage one another into our new identities. This is only possible by the work of the Spirit. This is also why joy and celebration are key characteristics of Spirit-filled worship. Knowing we are loved, knowing we are in the process of being healed and restored through Jesus's resurrection on the cross, causes us to sing and shout God's praises. As the Spirit was to Jesus, so he is to us – the author of deep joy: 'At that time, Jesus full of joy through the Holy Spirit, said, "I praise you Father, Lord of Heaven and Earth"' (Luke 10.21).

We have seen many salvations at Gas Street Church over the past five years. What is extraordinary is that most of them have come in our times of sung worship, not necessarily in our overt mission or evangelism. This tells us that worship is a powerful witness of the Father's love, displayed in the person of Christ, made powerfully experiential by the work of the Spirit in our midst. Our worship has been the welcome many have needed to step into the Father's house for the first time.

---

13 1 Peter 2.9.

At one gathering, I'll never forget the altar call being given and then a young student walking timidly forward to give her life to Jesus. Immediately, two other students who were part of our church got out of their seats and ran through the church to get to her. They scooped her up in a huge hug and danced in sheer delight. What an image of adoption and of the Spirit at work in our worship! I'm sure there was a whole heavenly host of classmates and saints cheering her on too.

Ephesians 2.18 says, 'Through Christ we have access *in one Spirit to the Father*' (Ephesians 2.18, italics added). What does it mean for our worship to say the Spirit enables us to be children of God? Well, what if we saw our times of worship as if we were a group of children at play in the Father's house? How would that change the way we think and what we do? Perhaps we'd become more comfortable with a bit of mess? Perhaps we'd be happier to try things and not worry if they didn't always work out? Perhaps we'd be okay with more physical expression in worship? Perhaps we'd be keener to have children present in our gathered worship to remind the adults as to what it is to have childlike faith and freedom?

Everyone contributes

Part of the key truth we learn from studying Paul's two chapters on worship and the Spirit in 1 Corinthians 12–14 is that the Spirit enables everyone's contributions to corporate worship:

> What then shall we say brothers and sisters? When you come together, each of you has a hymn, or a word of instruction, a revelation, a tongue or an interpretation. Everything must be done so that the church may be built up. (1 Corinthians 14.2)[14]

---

14 The implication in context of 1 Cor 14.26 is that the Spirit is *responsible for our worship* as we come together.

Paul is making it clear that the Spirit democratizes worship! The true beauty of collective worship lies, not in what happens on stage, but in the people's contributions by the power of the Spirit. In the words of the late, influential, Vineyard pastor, John Wimber, 'everyone gets to play'.[15] The gifts of the Spirit (which we'll discuss more in a moment) are one of the key ways this kind of worship happens. They are there as a gift from God for us as a corporate body to deepen our relationship with him and witness more effectively and powerfully to others.[16] As theologian Gordon Fee says, 'Paul did not understand the presence of the Spirit that did not also include . . . evidence of the Spirit's working.' Gathered worship, in this sense, is a fulfilment therefore of Moses's prayer in Numbers 11.29: 'I wish that all the Lord's people were prophets and that the Lord would put his Spirit on them!'[17]

What happens then, in this kind of atmosphere? In this 'spacious place' of true worship of Jesus, embraced by the Father, all empowered and made possible by the work of the Spirit? We get changed, and this is our final exploration of the Spirit's work in worship.

Transformation – the power to change

'And the Lord – who is the Spirit – makes us more and more like him as we are changed into his glorious image' (2 Corinthians 3.18, NLT).

As we celebrate and declare our identity as sons and daughters of God in worship, entering the reality of the risen life of Christ by the work of the Spirit, so we are transformed to look like the one we worship. This is the place of moving from 'life in the flesh'

---

15 *Everyone Gets to Play: John Wimber's Teachings and Writings on Life Together in Christ*, 2009, Ampelon Publishing.

16 Gordon Fee, *Paul, the Spirit, and the People of God*, Hendrickson Publishing, 1996, p. 166. If you'd like to read more about ministering the spiritual gifts, David Pytches book *Come Holy Spirit* is a helpful guide.

17 See Fee, p. 156.

to 'life in the Spirit', where our minds get reset on 'what the Spirit desires' (Romans 8.5–8). Our lives get reshaped towards true life and peace (8.6) that come from submitting to God and following the way of Jesus.[18] This is a fulfilment of the Old Testament hope expressed by Jeremiah, Ezekiel and others that God would internalize his 'law' – somehow put his very ways inside our hearts: 'I will give you a new heart and put a new spirit in you; I will remove from you your heart of stone and give you a heart of flesh'[19] (Ezekiel 36.26).

The Spirit in our times of worship facilitates this process happening deep within us. This transforming work can be in our character and lifestyle choices (the 'fruits' of the Spirit from Galatians 5.22 – love, joy, peace, patience, kindness, goodness, faithfulness, gentleness and self-control) or in our decision-making, will and vision for the future. As already mentioned, it can deepen our relationship with Christ through some of the gifts of the Spirit, such as the gift of tongues and the prophetic.[20] It can also be an equipping or empowering for mission – the boldness seen filling the disciples to speak the gospel in Acts, or some of the other gifts of the Spirit, such as words of knowledge and healing.

In my own life, I have found the atmosphere of the people of God at worship to be the most life-giving, life-changing place. So many key decisions, crucial character changes, increases in faith, and overall confidence to minister and lead others to Christ have happened in the midst of my worshipping with others. I remember the moment the Spirit gave me the gift of tongues as I sang in the middle of a congregation of teenagers at a Youth With A Mission Summer Camp – the English words were no longer enough, and a whole new heavenly language emerged which just poured out praises to God. I had the

---

18 The Holy Spirit is in fact the power we need to turn from the hold of sin. (Romans 8.13).

19 See Jeremiah 31.31–4 and Ezekiel 37.14.

20 The gifts of the Spirit 'aid us in praise' (Fee, p. 153).

overall sense of what I was expressing but not the precise meaning. It transformed my intimacy with God and remains a key fuel of my prayer life today. I remember the Spirit speaking to me so clearly in a time of worship that I was to pursue working for the church in full-time ministry. It was like a bolt of lightning, so clear and so power-ful a call in my heart. It wasn't audible, but it was just as real, just as life-changing a moment, as if a human had spoken directly to me.

Perhaps my biggest transformation was the one I opened this chapter with – going from being someone who never sang in pub-lic to being a worship leader! I was utterly changed by the Holy Spirit. Not just a temporary transformation, but a lifelong re-alter-ation of my perspective, aspirations and desires. I suddenly want-ed, as the Psalmist writes, to 'dwell in the house of the Lord all the days of my life, to gaze on the beauty of the Lord and seek him in his temple' (Psalm 27.4). I suddenly would do anything to be in and around the people of God worshipping. There was an atmosphere there, a sweetness, beauty and powerful reality that I found intox-icating. I now understood what the Psalmist meant when he said he'd rather be a gatekeeper – even on the edge of the worshipping people – than in the very best location the world could offer (Psalm 84.10). In fact, I spent one summer stewarding at worship events just to be near the presence of the Holy Spirit in worship. What I had experienced through starting to sing was freedom. The kind of inner expansive change that can only come from the Spirit of God.

Cosmic change

This personal transformation that occurs in our worship should be understood theologically as part of a much bigger *cosmic* transfor-mation that the Spirit is doing. He is 'perfecting'[21] the work begun

---

21 A term used to describe the Spirit by St Basil the Great – one of the early Church theologians and teachers.

and enacted by the Father and the Son in creation and salvation. As we worship, the Spirit is restoring the Father's original intent for the world through the death and resurrection of his son, and we are caught up in that work as we worship. English theologian Colin Gunton puts it like this: 'Through (Jesus), God re-establishes our life in its orientation to its promised perfection . . . The directness of our life is now determined . . . by the pull of the Spirit to completion rather than the pull of sin to dissolution.'[22]

The 'supernormal'

If we are to understand the Spirit's role in worship as restoring things to how they were supposed to be, according to the Father's design and the Son's sacrifice on the cross, then the Spirit's work in worship can be described not so much as the 'supernatural' but the 'supernormal'. If our sin and turning from God makes our own lives and our world misshapen, unfulfilled, and damaged, then the Holy Spirit transforms and restores us to the shape we were intended to be, the flourishing 'life to the full' Jesus spoke of for us (John 10.10). Our times of gathered worship can therefore be spiritually charged atmospheres and yet led in very down-to-earth, accessible manner. This is how intimacy and accessibility can be held together in tension as key values for our worship.

The Spirit's activity in and through us as we worship is also how we can understand the 'now and not yet' of the kingdom coming. As theologian James Torrance puts it, 'Jesus Christ is present in the power of the Spirit, but the same Spirit keeps us in suspense. The end is not yet.'[23] Having a deep biblical understanding of the work of the Holy Spirit in worship gives us the confidence to lean into the

---

22 Colin E. Gunton, *The Actuality of Atonement: A Study of Metaphor, Rationality, and the Christian Tradition*, Grand Rapids, Mich.: W.B. Eerdmans, 1989, p.167.

23 James Torrance, *Worship, Community, and the Triune God of Grace*, Carlisle: Paternoster Press, 1996, p. 82.

renewing, transforming work of the Spirit, while holding a mature cross-shaped understanding of the mystery, and often pain, of the waiting for full restoration and completion that the Spirit will only enact at the end of time.

All of this Spirit-empowered transformation in worship, the experiential manifestations of the Spirit, should, of course, not ultimately be understood in an individualistic, 'therapeutic' category but in a corporate 'missional' understanding of the Spirit's end goal and the Church's purpose. We are gifted with the Spirit's presence and power, not for our own blessing (although receiving anything from the Spirit *is* an experience of the gracious love of God for us), but so that we can be a blessing to others. We are filled so as to display the person, power and love of God to those we meet, live with and work alongside. The Spirit works in worship so we can better witness to the world and therefore glorify God.

Closing thoughts

Given the extraordinary work of the Spirit in worship, it is crucially important that we ensure that our collective worship is consciously *Spirit-dependent* – regardless of what particular outward form it may take. Our worship is a vessel for the living power and purposes of God to be enacted and displayed through the people of God – not only in that moment of collective praise, but with powerful consequences for our places of work, business and family decisions and interactions with neighbours and friends.

It is no wonder that, over a century ago, Charles Spurgeon felt so strongly about the need for the Holy Spirit to be prayed for and given space:

Friends, if we do not have the Spirit of God, it would be better to shut the churches, to nail up the doors and put a black cross on them and say, 'God have mercy on us!' If you ministers have not the Spirit of God, you had better not preach, and you people had better stay at home. I think I speak not too strongly when I say that the church in the land without the Spirit of God is rather a curse than a blessing. This is a solemn word: the Holy Spirit or nothing and worse than nothing.[24]

Praying and planning for the Spirit's work in our worship postures the church towards offering the world a place of living water, a living community that displays the mystery and majesty of the unrivalled God, revealed fully in his son Jesus. When Jesus stood up in the public square in John 7.37, he offered everyone a drink – of living water, the Spirit of God: 'Let anyone who is thirsty come to me and drink!' We, his Church, must do the same – every time, everywhere, for everyone. Come Holy Spirit.

Further resources for digging deeper

Nick J. Drake – *A Deeper Note*
Simon Ponsonby – *More*
Jim Cymbala – *Fresh Wind, Fresh Fire*
David Pytches – *Come Holy Spirit*
Graham Tomlin – *The Prodigal Spirit*
Gordon Fee – *Paul, the Spirit, and the People of God*
Tom Smail – *The Giving Gift*
Cath Woolridge – *Pylon People: 40 Days of Art and Meditations to Empower Your Spirit – a Creative Journal*
Theresa Berger and Bryan D. Spinks – *The Spirit in Worship-Worship in the Spirit*

---

24 Charles H Spurgeon quoted in R.T. Kendall, *Word and Spirit: Truth, Power, and the Next Great Move of God*.

Part 2

WHERE AND HOW
WE WORSHIP

Having spent time reflecting on the nature of God himself, Father, Son and Holy Spirit, in this section, we're going to focus on embedding worship in our lives – individually, corporately and in our day-to-day work. Worship is not only a response to what God has done for us, but a way of partnering with God in being his presence and his people on earth. We can only partner with him if we pursue a healthy integration of our worship – the private, the (gathered) public and the (scattered) 'public square'. In fact, we can only fulfil God's calling on our lives to be a city on a hill, a light that cannot be hidden, if we faithfully worship him and prioritize his ways in everything we do.

We begin by opening the door on the 'private' space of our lives. How do we invest in our own personal devotion? What are some of the crucial tools to help us worship when no one is looking? This is the first question we explore, and Graham Kendrick is the perfect guide. Having spent so much of his career 'up front' as a worship leader and songwriter, personal worship has been a key source of sustenance and strength for him. In this chapter, Graham encourages us to develop rhythms of worship in our day-to-day lives that will last a lifetime. He invites us to be 'self-starters', not depending on others to lead us but rather leading ourselves first and foremost to live authentic, sustained lives of worship.

If we foster good devotional practices in our own lives, when we come together to worship, how much more powerful and authentic will our praises be? This is the topic of Chapter 6, which Lou Fellingham brilliantly leads us through. Why come together to worship and sing? What does singing do? How is physical expression linked to worshipping together? How does worship foster a greater sense of community? She ends by inspiring us to come to corporate worship with faith and expectation: 'as you lift your voice, as you declare truth again over your life, as you lay your worries before him, God will meet with you!'

The final chapter of this section focuses on being a follower of Jesus in the scattered world. Worship must never be merely something we do on a Sunday and then 'switch off', but a posture, a priority and a purpose we carry with us into whatever area of life and work God has called us into. Lyn Weston from the London Institute for Contemporary Christianity expertly leads us through themes such as worship and justice, and how worship must overflow into action, as well as offering some really practical guidance for being a fruitful Christian in our everyday life. She leaves us with the challenge: 'What is happening in the 110 hours a week where we are not worshipping at church? How do we worship God in those places?'

DR NICK DRAKE

5

Worshipping on our own

GRAHAM KENDRICK

Graham is often described as a 'father of modern worship music', and for more than 30 years he has been writing and recording songs that have become modern classics. Based in the UK, Graham travels around the world participating in tours, festivals, conferences and training events, as a worship leader, speaker and performer, as well as being an advocate of Compassion International.

One of my earliest memories is of climbing into the back seat of our family car and watching my dad start it up – from outside the vehicle! He would pick up a steel crank handle from the car floor, walk around and engage the end in a slot in the front of the engine. Then, bending his whole body to the task, he would vigorously rotate the engine until it spluttered into life. Or didn't . . . Sometimes he would have to remove his jacket, roll up the sleeves of his shirt and try it again. We would all break into a cheer when it started, and he would have to jump in quickly and start driving before it stalled and he had to start again. Today, that model of car is considered a valuable classic; back then, it was just an old banger. It clearly predated the useful innovation of the electric starter motor, which serves to illustrate a simple question. When it comes to offering worship to God, am I a self-starter, or do I depend on someone else's muscle? Do I only worship when gathered with others and led by someone, or will I worship God any time, any place?

As human beings, we are wired for worship. We can't help it. In a sense, we are always worshipping something. It's not a case of *will we* worship but *what will we* worship? We are created to love and worship our Creator, and in his absence we feel a kind of cosmic loneliness and will try almost anything to fill the emptiness inside. An emptiness we most often feel when we stop, because this is when what lies below the busyness of our lives begins to surface. Anxieties, questions, regrets, numbness, boredom, anger, loneliness, fear, habits that demand to be satisfied. The wild animals of our unruly thoughts begin to gather at the waterhole of our subconscious minds. There are so many ways to stave these things off, but perhaps none so powerful and pervasive as our smartphones. For most of us, this little screen has become the hub of our life, and it's capable of shaping our attitudes, our desires, our politics, our beliefs. We never have to be silent or at rest or alone. Have a two-minute wait for a friend? We turn to our phone. Bored by what we're watching on TV? We turn to our phone. Walking down the street and have some headspace to fill? We turn to our phone. But it is a false friend. It gets to know all about us, our desires and fears; then, just at our most vulnerable moments, it offers to satisfy them – for a price. We, the user, have become the product. Unless we take charge of our inner lives and keep our focus on God, turning our hearts and our minds towards him through worship, prayer, reading our Bibles and waiting in silence to listen for God's voice, we will be no more than disciples of the secularized culture around us.

Often we're most tempted to distract ourselves when what we really, really need is communion with God. We are tempted to these lesser consolations instead, but let's not forget that consolation prizes are to cheer up the loser, not to reward the winner! There is something so much better for us. Something that will truly satisfy.

When Jesus spoke to a Samaritan woman at Jacob's well, he told her that she only had to ask and he would give her living water. This living water was such that she would never thirst again. As he spoke these words about the Holy Spirit, the promise was to all those who drink. Not just a once-only drink, but a constant spring welling up inside. But are we drinking deeply from it or just sipping occasionally? How do we disconnect from all the distractions and worship God with our all?

The secret worshipper

In the flow of some of Jesus's most famous teaching, the Beatitudes, recorded in Matthew's Gospel, he paints vivid pictures of the kind of worshipper he wants his disciples to be (6.1–6, 16–18). It might come as a surprise because he suggested that his listeners shut themselves in a cupboard. It also involved some confidential accounting and a careful check in the mirror before leaving the house. He starts by taking it for granted that his disciples will have three life habits: 'When you give . . . when you pray . . . when you fast.' Probably no one in his audience would have blinked at that; for them, it was religion 101. He goes on to describe how *not* to do those, using the religious elite of the day, the Pharisees, as a bad example. Why? Because they took those good actions and put on a show in order to impress. But, as for his disciples, he wanted them to do it very differently. Middle Eastern homes had very little private space, but there would generally be a small storeroom a person could squeeze into and shut the door. 'Go there,' he says. 'Be a secret worshipper.'

What a beautiful invitation to intimacy. He wants his disciples to pray, to give and to fast in secret where only our father in heaven can see. Surely this is more than simply a wise safeguard against spiritual pride; rather, it is God the Father's invitation to a secret worship life. That secret place inside our hearts and heads, where our innermost feelings, desires, hopes and fears surface, this is the very place that God desires to transform into a place of intimate communion with himself. He's not put off by the true state of our hearts, our unhealed pain and our unresolved issues. He wants to get to that place where we're real about our God-given human needs, hopes and longings. This is the very place where we can drink from the spring of living water and slake the deep thirsts of the soul.

We, of course, can't spend our entire lives in this secret place, but our public life and our public worship should flow from this secret worship life. If we're worshipping alone, how much more powerful the worship when we come back together! How refreshing it would be if worship songs or prayers broke out spontaneously in the congregation before even a note was played or anyone stepped up to a microphone. A room full of Spirit-filled self-starters is an awesome thing.

Those who have taken the words of Psalm 103 to heart: 'Praise the Lord, my soul; *all* my inmost being, praise his holy name' (italics added) know that worship starts with the will, the will that decides to engage the 'all'. And until we each exercise our choice routinely in our daily lives and private spaces, we will be leaning too much on the 'muscle' of the good people who lead us in the public setting. Don't wait for a feeling, make a choice. Don't wait for others to stir you up, stir yourself. Don't wait to be in church before you worship, worship wherever you are.

Forming spiritual habits

It is easy today, when we have so much wonderful music and so many great songs, to think that worship is all about singing to God. In fact, the songs are not the worship. They are simply vehicles to express our hearts, emotions and wills, giving us words and melodies that catch the overflow of our daily walk with God. These spiritual habits – or disciplines, as they are sometimes called – are key to creating and sustaining our day-to-day relationship with God when the music stops.

During my twenties, I spent two and a half years as a member of a travelling mission team. In our youthful zeal, we were rather proud of the long hours we worked and how little sleep we could survive on. Fortunately, wisdom and good advice prevailed, and we began to schedule days off. My problem was I didn't know how to relax or wind down in a positive way, let alone how to recharge spiritually. My days off were write-offs, and as the adrenaline of activity drained out of my body, I felt depressed and empty. My spiritual life had come to revolve around the demands of ministry, but when I was alone, I had nowhere to go, no solid habits or disciplines to fall back on.

There was no sudden turnaround, but over a number of years, I established several core habits to underpin my wobbly 'house of prayer'. They turned out to be pretty much the basics most of us know about but struggle to actually do! The first thing to do was to fix a time, find a place and establish a pattern. My lifestyle has never been routine – more of a constant juggling of family commitments, frequent travels and creative projects – so I learnt to live by the mantra 'do it first'. I had to start to seize the day even as it began. Of course, there are seasons when life's responsibilities are very demanding; for example, babies and children tend to seize the day before you are even fully conscious! It certainly didn't happen every day, but to tiptoe out of the sleeping house and walk and pray for a while was a lifeline for me for many years. Walking is also an effective antidote to falling asleep in a chair!

I grew up in a church culture that made a virtue out of spiritual spontaneity and so was suspicious of written liturgies and spiritual routines that went by the calendar or the clock. There has since been a much-needed restoration of respect for such patterns, many of which are ancient. The trouble with spontaneity is that, by definition, it may or may not happen! It depends a lot on our moods, our physical and spiritual energies and on the people and things around us that have their own 'spontaneity' that can interrupt our best intentions.

To fix a regular time or times for private prayer is a great beginning, but why not aspire to embrace the very rhythms of life – morning and evening, light and darkness, summer and winter, mealtimes, waking and sleeping and so on – as living, moving patterns for prayer? Many monasteries established such rhythms and created beautiful prayers and praises which are available to us to this day.

For one season of my life, my 'prayer cupboard' was a playing field which I would circle early in the morning until it was time to return home. At other times, it would be my car; if I needed to sit with my Bible open, I would drive to a quiet place and park. Where could your prayer cupboard be?

At times I sought out someone in my local circle for a regular early prayer shift, perhaps once a week or whenever both diaries allowed. Just having such an arrangement was motivational, and the kingdom of God is such that blessings seem to be multiplied when 'two or three gather together in my name'. Today, through the power of the internet, your prayer partner could be almost anywhere.

We have a tendency to wish for perfect conditions, but they rarely exist, so we have to improvise and do the best with what we have. It is not a bad thing to have to struggle a little for a time and place to pray, as it tests our resolve. How many of us, given ideal conditions, might not actually make use of them? Not enough time? Ask yourself what you *do* make time for. (Maybe check your phone usage record!) Perhaps we already have all we need if only we opened our eyes.

The biggest rebuke to my excuses has to be the famous example of Susanna Wesley, mother of the legendary John and Charles Wesley. With ten children to care for, her house was never quiet, but she had committed to spending time each day in prayer and Bible study. Even in the busiest years of her life, she made sure she spent two hours each day with God. How did she find privacy and peace in a house that full? Susanna would sit in her favourite chair, Bible in hand, and throw her long apron over her head like a tent. Everyone in the house knew not to disturb her unless it was an emergency.[1]

---

1 <www.faithgateway.com/praying-example-susanna-wesley/#.XylE455KhPY>

A Bible reading plan

Once we have set aside time alone with God, we can pick up our Bibles. But this can be daunting, in the least; where do I start, how can I make it a habit? My haphazard Bible reading at last took better shape when I was given what was, at the time, a new type of Bible. It had been split into 365 daily readings that allowed you to read through the whole book in one year. This format, of course, has become a staple with many 'Bible in One Year' reading plans available. The most frequently used format is that each day you read a chunk of Old Testament, New Testament, a Psalm and a Proverb. Each day's reading is about 20 minutes long, and I've kept with this format ever since. It gives me a simple and logical structure and means I always know what to read next. It also introduced me to passages I had rarely, if ever, read because my Bible reading had not previously been systematic or comprehensive.

I would highly recommend that method, but overall there has never been such a great variety of Bible reading schemes, daily meditations and the like, be it short, long, academic, popular, available in numerous translations and paraphrases, paperback, leather-bound, online, offline, interactive and so on. Let's pick at least one that helps us form a Bible reading habit (you'll find some suggestions at the end of this chapter) and, as a certain brand of sportswear boldly proclaims, just do it!

Singing from your 'inner songbook'

Sometimes I wake up to find a song I know inside my head. Sometimes it is a half-remembered fragment that takes a while to identify, but I take it seriously and offer it back in worship and let it speak to me. Some people love to plug in earphones and worship with their playlist. Others I know keep a hymn book with their Bible and use them side by side. In my early days of faith, it seemed there was always a song of worship playing in my heart which would move to my lips when I was driving, walking or doing a routine task. I cannot overestimate how much this helped me to keep my attention fixed on the presence of God. Listening to worship music is such a blessing, but don't forget about 'making melody to the Lord *in your hearts*' (Ephesians 5.19, italics added). I'm not talking about song-writing or performance here. Now and again, turn off other people's worship and let your own rise up, whether a known song or just singing your prayers, however croaky or unmusical it may sound first thing in the morning! God listens for the music of the heart, and I'm pretty sure he will absolutely love it.

A daily prayer liturgy

This is not only for people from a liturgical background. Today, Christians from diverse traditions are discovering the value of the carefully constructed patterns of prayer, responses, Bible readings, creeds, etc., which comprise liturgy, in which rich biblical themes unfold through the year. It is generally understood to be a communal act, so why have I included it? The obvious answer is that by participating with the same words, we can worship with others without necessarily being in the same physical space. Some online liturgy apps include audio, so you can hear the voices of others as you join in. Explore the resources listed at the end of this chapter and try one for, say, a week.

Praying the Psalms

I love the book of Psalms. I have read them regularly, composed songs from them and spontaneously sung them straight from the page for many years. Even so, I think I am only just beginning to wake up to their immense power and significance. I love to open up a good commentary and learn about them from a scholar, but something remarkable starts to happen when I open up my mouth and wrap my lips, tongue and heart around the words and pray them aloud.

For me, the most inspiring fact about the Psalms is that they were Jesus's songbook and prayer book. He knew them inside out, sang them, prayed them, quoted them and even prayed them during the agonies of the crucifixion. These psalms have lasted thousands of years, been translated into multiple languages and were a staple diet for our spiritual ancestors. For centuries, our Christian brothers and sisters have lived and died with Psalms on their lips. They have served to voice the highs and lows of the human experience for century after century. It's pretty awe-inspiring when you think about it.

Athanasius (a theologian and leader in the early church) said that whereas most of Scripture speaks *to* us, the Psalms speak *for* us. They give us a language, a vocabulary of prayerful and worshipful engagement with God for every kind of circumstance and condition. There are many songs today that give us an excellent language for expressing our personal love and thanks to God, but the Psalms also give us a language for anger, for lament, for protesting against injustice and a language of hope for the future. We need to rediscover some of this language in our worship today that allows the Christian community to grieve, protest, lament, and anticipate God's final victory. Walter Brueggemann, in his excellent little book *Praying the Psalms,* says 'The Psalter knows that life is dislocated. No cover-up is necessary. The Psalter is a collection over a long period of time of the eloquent, passionate songs and prayers of people who are at the desperate edge of their lives.'[2]

So how do we pray the psalms?

One of the best ways is simply to read them out loud, but not in a detached, cerebral way. The book of Psalms begins with a promise that

---

2   Walter Brueggemann, *Praying the Psalms*, Authentic Media, 2007, 2nd edition, 9.

the person who meditates on the law of the Lord is like 'a tree planted by streams of water, which yields its fruit in season and whose leaf does not wither. Whatever he does prospers' (Psalm 1.3). That is quite a promise. Meditation sounds like a purely mental activity, but, according to Eugene Peterson, to 'meditate (hagah) is a bodily action; it involves murmuring and mumbling words, taking a kind of physical pleasure in making the sounds of the words, getting the feel of the meaning as the syllables are shaped by larynx and tongue and lips.'[3] The Psalms spring to life when we engage with them physically. Try it!

As familiarity with them grows, we will find that remembered psalm phrases or fragments become ingrained in our memories to fuel our spontaneous prayer and worship – a rich resource for the Holy Spirit to prompt prayer and praise, as a defence against sin (Ps 119.11) and in moments of crisis. Eugene Peterson points out that Jonah's psalm-like prayer in the belly of the whale (Jonah 2.2–9) was not original; its component parts can be traced back to at least 10 sources in the Psalms. It was an inspired 'mash-up'! He had worked out at 'psalm gym' and so, in a moment of desperation, he had a vocabulary of prayer to draw upon. As psalm phrases lodge in our memories, they reshape our view of God and our circumstances, enabling us to make the connection between our human condition and God's priorities, purposes and provisions for us. Whereas my own prayer vocabulary becomes exhausted or narrow, or the issue looms so large that my faith falters, a psalm can very quickly open up God's perspective and agenda.

If you would like to try singing the Psalms, visit <www.graham-kendrick.co.uk/psalmsurfing> for ideas to get you started.

Scripture statements

There's something incredibly powerful about taking the statements of Scripture and turning them into spoken declarations

---

3 Eugene Peterson, *Answering God*, Marshall Pickering, 1996, 26.

over our lives. I'm not suggesting we quote words of Scripture as a formula to get what we want from God, rather to declare the truth of what we already have in Jesus in the light of all he achieved on the cross. For example, 'Therefore, if anyone is in Christ, the new creation has come: the old has gone, the new is here!' (2 Corinthians 5.17). Simply insert the personal pronoun and make it yours: 'I am a new creation in Christ, the old has gone, the new is here!' Or do the same with truths such as: 'For we are God's handiwork, created in Christ Jesus to do good works, which God prepared in advance for us to do' (Ephesians 2.10). Or 'His divine power has given us everything we need for a godly life through our knowledge of him who called us by his own glory and goodness' (2 Peter 1.3).

Collect them, especially those that have been foundational in your spiritual life, and keep them with you, praying them often and declaring, 'This is who I am in Christ!' Obsessing over our shortcomings and failures is a pathway to despair, but having confessed our weaknesses and sins, it's important to then reorient ourselves by declaring the truth of what God has done for us in Christ. As with the Psalms, I find it helpful to do this out loud as it engages me in a deeper way.

Monastic practices

There are several monastic practices that have much to teach us about connecting with God in the secret place, turning our eyes from the world and focusing on him. Here is an overview of a few that you may wish to learn more about and practice.

Lectio Divina

Lectio Divina dates back hundreds of years and can be translated 'sacred reading'. It's a way of praying and contemplating scriptures so as to allow God to speak to us today. It encourages us to slow down, repeatedly reading a passage in order to savour it and to encounter God as its author. It can be done alone or in a group, and there are many resources online that can guide you through how to do it. As a simple outline, the Lectio Divina encourages us to spend some time in quiet to still our thoughts before we:

1 Read a verse or two – slowly and repeatedly.
2 Reflect – between each reading, asking the Holy Spirit what he wants to say to you today.
3 Respond – how do you want to respond to this in prayer?
4 Rest – allowing space for the word of God to dwell in you richly.

The 24-7 Prayer movement has a Lectio365 app, and you'll also find plenty of helpful resources online.

The Examen

The Examen is another monastic tradition that can be a helpful habit to explore today. It's often best practiced at the end of the day and is a time of reflection and self-examination, looking to detect God's presence in the day gone by and to discern his voice and presence.

St Ignatius practiced these five steps:

1 Become aware of God's presence.
2 Review the day with gratitude.
3 Pay attention to your emotions.
4 Choose one feature of the day and pray from it.
5 Look toward tomorrow.

You may wish to discover more of this tradition by looking online or to employ those simple steps by taking time at the end of each day to sit before God and see if there is unconfessed sin to be dealt with or worries and anxieties that need to be laid down.

Silence and listening

As I said at the start of this chapter, we are addicted to information and noise, continually overloading our senses; we have lost our ability to be quiet. Someone I know signed up to spend several days on his first silent retreat. Settling into his room, he pitched in enthusiastically and prayed himself dry. Looking at his watch, he was horrified to find that he had only used up about 15 minutes of the long hours of solitude and silence that stretched out before him!

Time and space to be quiet is countercultural and may take some practice. If we need a reminder of how important it is, we can just look at the fact that Jesus regularly withdrew from others to spend time with his Father. If the Son of God needed this, how much more do we? As we quieten down, what is really going on begins to rise to the surface. We begin to bring our true selves before our Father, letting go our own agendas and making space for him to speak to us. We can worship without words, our hearts in awe of God, offering him all we have in the simplicity of our silence.

Worshipping with our minds

These Bible-soaked disciplines and habits are so effective at helping us to worship God with our minds. Jesus summed up what God requires in this way, 'Love the Lord your God with all your heart and with all your soul and with all your strength and with all your mind,' and, 'Love your neighbour as yourself' (Luke 10.27).

Our culture is so focussed on feelings and experience that we can easily downgrade the 'all your mind' category. Paul urges the Romans:

> In view of God's mercy, to offer your bodies as a living sacrifice, holy and pleasing to God – this is your true and proper worship. Do not conform to the pattern of this world but be transformed by the renewing of your mind. Then you

will be able to test and approve what God's will is – his good, pleasing and perfect will. (Romans 12.1–2)

As we allow the Holy Spirit to search our secret thoughts, as we repent of what we discover grieves him, then we are better able to think as Paul exhorted the Philippian believers to: 'Finally, brothers, whatever is true, whatever is noble, whatever is right, whatever is pure, whatever is lovely, whatever is admirable if anything is excellent or praiseworthy think about such things' (Philippians 4.8).

Guard the wellspring of your heart

'Above all else, guard your heart, for everything you do flows from it' (Proverbs 4.23). What wise counsel that is! All I have said, which is only a fraction of what can be said on the subject, is a step towards doing this. The inner life flows out and shapes our behaviour, our priorities, our relationships – for better or worse. Miroslav Volf said 'Christian worship consists both in obedient service of God and in joyful praise of God . . . authentic Christian worship takes place in a rhythm of adoration and action.'[4] The secret place of worship is where we set the tempo of the outward worship actions such as: 'Be joyful always; pray continually; give thanks in all circumstances, for this is God's will for you in Christ Jesus'

(1 Thessalonians 5.16–18).

That rhythm is where life and lips agree, where actions are as truly offerings of worship as our public witness and our songs of praise and adoration. Hebrews 13.15 reminds us that both verbal professions of Christ and loving actions are described equally as sacrifices of praise. 'Through Jesus, therefore, let us continually offer to God a sacrifice of praise – the fruit of lips that openly profess his name.

---

4   Miroslav Volf, "Worship as Adoration and Action: Reflections on a Christian Way of Being-in-the-World" in *Worship: Adoration and Action*, ed. D. A. Carson, 203, 207

And do not forget to do good and to share with others, for with such sacrifices God is pleased.'

One more 'whatever' opens up the whole-life nature of personal worship: 'and whatever you do, whether in word or deed, do it all in the name of the Lord Jesus, giving thanks to God the Father through him' (Colossians 3.17).

Start with small steps; don't give up! Expect your sinful nature to squeal and complain. If it sometimes seems dull and repetitive, so did cleaning your teeth when you were a little child but it was a worthwhile habit! Think of it as daily manna in the wilderness – tedious at times, but without it they could not have survived, let alone thrived.

Jesus says; 'Come to me, all you who are weary and burdened, and I will give you rest' (Matthew 11.28). Let us answer with the psalmist, 'My heart says of you, "Seek his face!" Your face, Lord, I will seek' (Psalm 27.8).

Further resources for digging deeper

Charlie Cleverly – *The Discipline of Intimacy: The Joy and Awe of Walking with God*
John Mark Comer – *The Ruthless Elimination of Hurry*
Walter Brueggemann – *Praying the Psalms*
Eugene Peterson – *Answering God: Psalms as Tools for Prayer*
Gerard Kelly – *Spoken Worship*
Gerard Kelly – *I See a New City: Poems of Place and Possibility* (Spoken Worship Book 2)
Graham Kendrick – *Worship*

Daily prayer apps

24-7 Lectio365 app
Common Worship 'Daily Prayer'

'Celebrating Common Prayer' (Franciscans)
The CofE 'Time to Pray'
The CofE 'Daily Prayer'
The CofE 'Lectionary'

6

Worshipping together

LOU FELLINGHAM

Lou has been at the heart of the UK worship music industry for the last 20 years as a songwriter and worship leader. She was the lead singer in the popular band Phatfish and has released seven solo albums. Her passion is to embody authenticity and spiritual integrity while communicating the power of the gospel and God's outrageous love.

Sunday morning: the alarm goes off; you hit the snooze button for the third time. You didn't sleep well, it's cold outside and you're struggling to find the motivation to get out of your comfy, warm bed. Eventually, you drag yourself to the kitchen only to find last night's washing up still on the side, the milk has run out and you're already running late. You shout at your children/spouse/housemate/cat because you're feeling the pressure and no one is doing what you want them to. Eventually, you're on your way and you reflect on your week. You've had some highs and lows, and you acknowledge that during the tougher moments, you've maybe not done so well at looking to God for comfort and instead have turned to other things. The guilt settles in your stomach; you're going to have to face people in a few minutes. You eventually charge into church, late, flustered, angry and full of shame, trying to put on a brave face and pretend that everything is fine.

This may be an exaggeration of your typical Sunday morning, but I'm sure some aspects will resonate with you! Sundays can be a struggle. We often walk through the church doors carrying a whole raft of physical, emotional and spiritual needs. The weight of the week has piled up and sometimes feels even heavier as we walk into the building and have to face people. And then, to top it all off, we have to . . . sing! I mean, what is that all about?

Why should we even meet together?

Well, first, because the Bible tells us to! Hebrews 10.24–25 says, 'And let us consider how to stir up one another to love and good works, not neglecting to meet together, as is the habit of some, but encouraging one another.'

Now this scripture is not a cold command but is one that recognizes meeting together will do us good. Gathering together shouldn't be something which adds to the burdens we are carrying or be a place where we have to paint on a shiny, happy 'everything is okay' smile. Rather, it's an opportunity to be encouraged by others as we cheer one another on. God has given us each other for mutual encouragement, and as we pour ourselves out towards each other in love, we can also experience the weights we are carrying being lifted.

This process of mutual encouragement happens with God in the midst of us. We no longer have to wait for specific moments or be in particular places to be able to draw near to and meet with God like the Old Testament saints. The priesthood of Christ which we read about in Hebrews is a 'better' priesthood than the one they experienced. David's longing and thirst to be in 'the courts of the Lord'[5] can be quenched, through Christ, at any time or place by the power of the Holy Spirit.

But does this take away the need for the corporate gathering when we think about 'drawing near to God'? The exhortations in Colossians and Ephesians to sing psalms, hymns and spiritual songs would suggest not. 1 Corinthians 14.26 clearly refers to gathered worship communities. The Psalms are filled with appeals like 'Come, let us sing for joy to the Lord; let us shout aloud to the Rock of our

5   Psalm 84:2

salvation. Let us come before him with thanksgiving and extol him with music and song' (Ps 95.1–2). This corporate journey depicted in the Psalms should have just as much potency now as it did when first written, only made richer by the finished work of Christ.

In a society that is all about individualism, self-sufficiency and self-glorification, God calls us to a different way. Yes, we have individual encounters with God, but we have been adopted into the family of God. We are invited into the very life of God. We become part of the body, joined together in Christ with him as the head. He cares about our coming together; we belong together. Working together. Caring for one another. Blessing one another. We are now called out of living for ourselves and drawn into living for Jesus. Meeting together is an important way to help us live out this truth.

In addition, when we gather together as God's people, we display to a watching world that Jesus is Lord and King over our lives. So our gathering is to God and for God in the company of fellow believers who are mutually edified and before a watching world that also desperately needs to know God's love and mercy.

What has singing got to do with it?

'Sing praises to God, sing praises! Sing praises to our King, sing praises!' (Psalm 47.6).

'Oh sing to the Lord a new song; sing to the Lord, all the earth. Sing to the Lord, bless his name; tell of his salvation from day to day' (Psalm 96.1–2).

In these four verses alone we're commanded to sing seven times, and the Psalms command us to sing over 40 times! And, other than church, few places remain where corporate singing is encouraged; chanting at a football stadium probably isn't what the psalmist was getting at. God made us to sing and, yes, that includes all of us, even those of us who squirm at the thought of it. If you're new to Christianity, it might seem like a strange concept! For some of us, we're embarrassed by our voices and would rather no one heard us, so we confine our singing to the shower. If, for whatever reason, you've decided singing is not for you, let me encourage you, urge you, even, that your voice has a place. Here are a few reasons why.

1 The Bible says nothing about singing only if you're suitably accomplished to do so.

Nowhere do we see the instruction 'Sing to the Lord all of you who are comfortable with it, and sit down quietly all of you who are wishing the floor would swallow you up.' There's no verse that says, 'Sing, you worship leaders, and the rest of you just watch.' I'm afraid not. Throughout the Bible, God calls us all to sing.

2 God is a singing God, and we are made in his image.

Zephaniah 3.17 depicts the eternal God delighting in his people as he rejoices over them with singing. This powerful scene has been described as 'a grand oratorio as God and his people mutually rejoice in their love for each other'.[1] What an incredible thought! We also read in the gospels that, after the last supper, Jesus sang a hymn together with his disciples. God sings!

3 Singing can be a means of teaching, being filled with the Spirit and filling us with joy.

Colossians 3.16 says 'Let the word of Christ dwell in you richly, teaching and admonishing one another in all wisdom, singing

---

1 O. Palmer Robertson, "The Book of Zephaniah", *The Books of Nahum, Habbakkuk, and Zephaniah*, (NICOT, Grand Rapids, Mich: Eerdmans 2005), Scribd Edition, Chapter 3.

psalms and hymns and spiritual songs, with thankfulness in your hearts to God.' There is a similar passage in Ephesians which says: 'And do not get drunk with wine, for that is debauchery, but be filled with the Spirit, addressing one another in psalms and hymns and spiritual songs, singing and making melody to the Lord with your heart' (Ephesians 5.18–19, ESV).

Songs are a wonderful way for us to learn; rhythm and melody are effective ways for us to remember truth. According to these scriptures, as we let the word of Christ dwell in us, as we sing and make melody to the Lord, we find that we are filled with the Spirit, which in turn causes thankfulness to rise up, resulting in joy filling our hearts. God knows that singing will do us good!

4 Singing can bring about transformation.

As we sing, we are being filled with the Spirit, and 'where the Spirit of the Lord is, there is also freedom' (2 Corinthians 3.17)! I love this scripture because it goes on to say that 'We all, with unveiled face, beholding the glory of the Lord are being transformed into the same image from one degree of glory to another. For this comes from the Lord who is the Spirit.'

God is transforming us, step by step, to become more like him; this is a work of the Spirit. The parallel passage in Colossians then emphasizes the Word of Christ dwelling in us richly as we sing. In Hebrews, we read that the Word is 'sharper than any double-edged sword, it penetrates even to dividing soul and spirit, joints and marrow; it judges the thoughts and attitudes of the heart.' As we sing out our songs, transformation can take place through the filling of the Spirit and the empowering, revealing Word of God.

5 Singing can give us an opportunity to express in song what we sometimes can't express in other contexts.

We can sometimes feel stuck with how to express our worship to God or not know what words to use. Well-written songs are great tools for us in these moments and help us connect and awaken our hearts and minds to the truth we need in our souls.

The good news is that there isn't just one type of song or sound. We can have all sorts of styles and accompaniments to use as tools to express the depths of our hearts. Sometimes it's a lament, sometimes it's a party, sometimes it's a proclamation, sometimes it's exclamation or a declaration. There's a time for each.

6 Singing together builds community

There is something that happens as we join together, singing the same song with one voice, that deepens our sense of belonging and being part of something together. Bob Kauflin puts it like this, 'Our singing tends to bind us together. It's more effective than simply reciting or shouting words in unison. Singing enables us to spend extended periods of time communicating the same thoughts, the same passions, and the same intentions. That process can actually have a physical effect on our bodies. Scientists have found that singing corporately produces a chemical change in our bodies that contributes to a sense of bonding.'[2]

Over the years, I have led in many different places with varying sizes of congregations and have experienced just this. There is one moment that particularly comes to mind. We

2   Bob Kauflin – <www.desiringgod.org/messages/words-of-wonder-what-happens-when -we-sing>

were in Canada at the time. It was an evening celebration, and the room was filled with men and women from around the city and across several denominations. We began with a corporate time of worship, and as hearts and voices were lifted around the room, there was a sense of expectation about what God was going to do that night. As we continued to sing, one of the ladies on the team sang out a prophetic song. It was a song about unity, based on Psalm 133. As she was singing, a pastor from one of the churches stood up and publicly repented of his attitude towards the other churches in the city, confessing that he had not been giving them the honour and respect that he should. His wife stood up and followed suit, leading to many other men and women also repenting of their sin and attitudes towards other pastors and churches. It was an extremely powerful, moving, transforming, deep work of the Spirit. We then continued the meeting, and the Holy Spirit moved powerfully throughout the night.

This is just one of the many occasions I have experienced being in a room where we lifted our voices in song together, fixed our attention on God and lives were changed (2 Cor 3.18).

Ingredients for corporate worship – revelation and response

So we've considered the importance of meeting together and the specific place of singing within that context, but what are the ingredients that our corporate worship should contain? Matt Redman helpfully talks about the rhythm of revelation and response being key to our corporate times together. We need to be filled with revelation of who God is and what he has done for us through singing songs which teach us and paint a grand picture of who God is and his work of salvation in our lives. We also need an opportunity to respond – to breathe out. If we have a diet full of revelation with no opportunity to respond, we can end up like a pressure cooker with the lid shut tight! But we also need songs which make it clear what we're responding to, so that our worship is not just driven by subjectivity.

Revelation

Without revelation from God, humanity could never find its way to him under its own initiative. God has revealed himself in the creation that we see all around us and then crystallized that revelation through his Word. When Jesus came to earth, he was the full image and revelation of God. John 16.13–15 tells us that it is the Holy Spirit who guides us into all truth so it is important that as we come to worship, we ask the Holy Spirit to open our eyes to see Jesus, to understand the heart and nature of God and to cause the Word to come alive to us.

The Bible shows us that it is all too easy for us to have a false understanding of God – take these two examples:

Worshipping who we do not know

When talking to the Samaritan woman at the well (John 4), Jesus said, 'Believe me, a time is coming when you will worship the Father neither on this mountain nor in Jerusalem. You Samaritans worship what you do not know; we worship what we do know, for salvation is from the Jews' (21–22).

One of the things about the Samaritans was that they only considered the Pentateuch (the first five books of the Bible) as Scripture, not the rest of the Hebrew Bible. They had also probably been strongly influenced by Greek culture and other ideologies. They were essentially inadequately taught, and consequently they had some key facts wrong. Jesus didn't mince his words in telling her: 'You Samaritans worship what you do not know.' Whatever the intentions this woman had in asking how to rightly worship, the God she has in mind was not the true God – she worshipped who she did not know. Jesus invites her to drink from the water of life where she will never thirst again. He (the Word) revealed himself to her and then offered her 'living water' (the Spirit).

Worshipping a counterfeit

The second example is from the book of Exodus where we read that the Israelites had seen God perform mighty miracles. They had known him with them, guiding them day and night, but then the moment he was 'out of sight', they built a golden calf to worship instead. Aaron pronounced 'these are your Gods O Israel' (32.4). It's easy to wonder how the Israelites could have possibly turned so quickly from the true and living God to something fashioned with human hands! Until we remember, we're not that different . . . We are constantly being bombarded by different things vying to take the position of God in our lives. We're told that in order to be happy and fulfilled, you need to be wealthy, powerful, thin, fit, self-sufficient, intellectual and so on. That's where being reminded of truth is so important; it's so easy to forget the truth of God's story that we're invited into. Singing truth helps us to reorient ourselves, re-align our perspective and remember that Jesus is the Lord of our lives, not some counterfeit God or ideology.

Love not duty

Singing truth isn't just about recounting hard facts or doing things out of duty. The heart of the gospel is love that draws us into relationship with the Father, Son and Holy Spirit. The Trinity are always loving one another and giving glory to each other. God's heart is that we get drawn into that beautiful dance. What an incredible invitation!

God is not standing with his arms crossed, waiting for our response from a disinterested distance. He is not calling us to love him in a demanding and cold-hearted way. He knows that human beings are hardwired to worship and will inevitably do so one way or another. The only way this worship will bring us life is when it's directed towards him. He gladly invites us to drink deeply from the living water in order to give us fullness of life. So as we sing out the message of Christ which has been revealed to us by the Spirit, we are filled up and our hearts are awakened with affection for God again as we remember all he is and all he has done for us.

Response

If someone gives you a gift and you don't say thank you, that would be considered rude. Or if someone wins the gold medal at the Olympics but the crowd just looks on in silence, it would be really weird! To show gratitude and excitement about good things is normal. How much more then should we respond when we have this incredible, unique invitation to draw near to God and to know him? We are compelled to respond. We respond with our voices, we respond with our bodies, we respond with our whole selves.

Along with singing, body language is a wonderful way to express our thankfulness and adoration to God. Our posture speaks volumes. In human interactions, we know we are welcome if someone opens their arms to us. We know we have someone's attention if they are looking at us rather than around the room at what else is going on. Likewise, body language towards God is important. This might put some of you off even more than when talking about singing, but stay with me! When we consider the Hebrew language used when talking about praise and worship to God, it teaches us a lot about what the Bible sees as being an appropriate response.

Yadah – To revere or worship with extended hands. To hold out the hands. To throw a stone or arrow (Psalm 67.3).

Halal – To boast. To rave. To shine. To celebrate. To be clamorously foolish. (Psalm 149.3)

Zamar – To make music. To celebrate in song and music. To touch the strings or parts of a musical instrument. (Psalm 144.9)

Towdah – An extension of the hand. Thanksgiving. A confession. A sacrifice of praise. Thanksgiving for things not yet received. A choir of worshippers.

Barak – To kneel. To bless God (as an act of adoration). To praise. To salute. To thank.

Tehilla – A hymn. A song of praise. A new song. A spontaneous song. (Psalm 22.3)

Shabach – To address in a loud tone. To shout. To commend, glory and triumph. (Psalm 145.4)[3]

Last summer, I was leading worship at an event where each morning we'd start with corporate all-age worship. The challenge here is to engage the children while not losing the adults! God spoke to me about using some of these Hebrew words during this time together and to encourage us, as a church, to step out of our comfort zones and our usual demonstration of worship and see what God would do.

I have a friend called Nicola Pike who is great with spoken word, so each morning she took one of these words and explored its meaning through her spoken word pieces. This taught us, then inspired and encouraged us to respond to God in these ways. The first morning we looked at *Shabach* – to raise a shout. This wasn't about hyping ourselves up; this was about receiving revelation and then responding with a shout, so we did just that. We filled our mouths and our hearts with truth about God, and then we responded with a shout. It was amazing! Something was beginning to stir.

The next morning, we looked at *Tehilla* – singing a new song. There are so many times in the Bible where God calls us to sing a new song, but most of us disqualify ourselves from this, thinking we're not songwriters so we should leave it to the professionals.

---

3 "Holy Roar: 7 Words That Will Change The way you worship" by Chris Tomlin and Darren Whitehead.

What we did was start with the revelation of God as we picked up our Bibles. We turned to scripture and began to sing out those words to whatever tune came to mind. It didn't matter at that moment how good that tune was; there was power in simply taking those words and articulating them through our songs. That morning, the team felt that God had given us a word about voices being unlocked. That there were some people who had felt shut down or allowed themselves to be put on mute, but as they began to lift their voices in song, God was going to set their voices free. There was a significant response, and one lady said she had been completely unable to make a sound with her voice for three months. In that moment, something suddenly changed and she began to sing!

The next morning, we took the word *Halal* – to be foolish in our celebration. Now this really got people shifting nervously in their seats! Often when we come to God in worship, we have the things we feel comfortable doing and those that makes us cringe. You might be fine raising your hands, but dancing? No way! I know there are many reasons for that, and I recognize that not everyone feels comfortable moving their bodies and some of us have physical restrictions that we need to be sensitive to. For some of us, though, we're more than happy to dance, shout, to make noise and celebrate in other contexts, but when we get to church, we suddenly get inhibited! In the Psalms there is also a call to dance and to celebrate before God. As with singing, I don't believe I have read anywhere that you should only do it if you're a really fantastic mover! On the morning we led into dance, someone brought a word that as people began to dance, God was going to heal bodies. Guess what? God did just that! To help people relax, we started by all doing the 'dad dance' (getting a few kids up on stage to demonstrate!) – then we led into a time of worship and a moment of just going for it. As we let down our barriers, our frameworks that we had put in place for so long, God broke in and set bodies free! A woman who had had arthritis in her knees since she had been eleven was healed. We were filled with such joy and thanks to God for his kindness!

On the final morning, we considered *Barak,* which means to kneel. We took this one further and bowed. Not everyone could do it because of space or physical ability, but we tried and it was truly special. Sometimes when you allow your body to move to a different place, you get a different view. There was something very powerful as people bowed or lay on the floor before their King. God met with us again in such a moving way.

Focusing in on these words gave us the opportunity to really think about the ways we respond to God's revelation to us. When the truth of who God is and all he has done for us comes alive to us, why wouldn't we want to sing, shout, dance and kneel in response?

Your voice counts

God loves to meet with his people and show us more of who he is. He has instructed us to sing to him and to dance before him, not because it's what they used to do in the olden days, but because he knows it is good for us and will bring glory to him. God speaks to us through song but also through one another. Maybe God will reveal something to you while singing that you can sing out and share with others. Maybe you will have a new song that will bless someone else or articulate exactly what they are feeling in the moment. Maybe you will have a scripture you can share that will help someone else.

When we come together, we need to know that God wants to meet with us and he wants us to be an encouragement to one another. He has given us the tools in his word to receive revelation of who he is, which is brought alive to us by the Holy Spirit. I want to encourage you that your voice counts. Come to corporate gatherings with expectation that as you lift your voice, as you declare truth again over your life, as you lay your worries before him, God will meet with you. And as you pour into the lives of those around you, you will be mutually edified and built up as, together, your faith is strengthened, hope is found and God is glorified. As we lift the name of Jesus high, we get to experience his manifest presence, his glory and his power among us.

Further resources for digging deeper

Les Moir – *Missing Jewel: the Worship Movement that Impacted the Nations*

Dai Woolridge – *Poetry in Motion: 50 Daily Readings of 21st Century Psalms for Worship, Prayer and Performance*

Smith, James K. A. – *You are what you love: the spiritual power of habit*, 2016.

7

Worshipping all the time and everywhere

LYN WESTON

Lyn is the director of Church of England Relations at the London Institute of Contemporary Christianity (LICC), helping Anglican dioceses and churches develop a whole-life disciple-making culture and inspiring people to make a difference for Christ wherever they are. Before becoming a priest, she spent 27 years delivering major change projects in the banking industry, and then was the Director of Mission for the Diocese of Chester.

How does the worship we share in as a church community overflow into the different aspects of our lives throughout the week? What difference does following Jesus and being loved by him make to our ordinary, everyday lives? The truth is that, with Christ, there is no ordinary – every encounter, every task, every situation brims with divine possibility. So how would things change if we realized that our gathered worship has the power to shape us and then send us out into the world to worship all the time and everywhere?

As Romans 12.1–2 tells us, 'true and proper worship' is to offer ourselves as living sacrifices. *All* of our life is an act of worship. It is so much more than being together as a church community or singing and praying. Whether we are looking after our family, working, spending our money, enjoying time with friends, greeting our neighbour, gardening, cleaning the house, completing a business deal, operating on a patient in hospital, teaching children at school; anything and everything we do can be worship if we do it in God's power and strength, in a way that is true to God's way and that gives glory to him. Our places of worship are wherever we are on our frontlines throughout the week, the places where we connect with the people among whom God places us and where we are able to demonstrate the love and purposes of God to his world. No matter the people we're with and what we're doing, we can all worship God every moment of every day.

Authentic gathered worship equips us to be scattered into God's world to make a difference wherever we are

When we think about worship, what usually springs to mind is sung worship; when we meet, however, what we hear from the Old Testament prophets puts emphasis on how we live our lives and worship *outside* gatherings. Israel's failure to practice justice outside their assemblies makes the worship inside their assemblies offensive to God, whose heart is for righteousness, justice, kindness and humility. Scripture teaches that if worshippers fail to practice justice in our everyday lives, then our worship lacks authenticity.

I despise your festivals, and I take no delight in your solemn assemblies. Even though you offer me your burnt offerings and grain offerings, I will not accept them; and the offerings of well-being of your fatted animals I will not look upon. Take away from me the noise of your songs; I will not listen to the melody of your harps. But let justice roll down like waters, and righteousness like an ever-flowing stream. (Amos 5.21–24)

The gathered worship of these people was dynamic, with offerings received, vibrant singing and rich prayers, so it must have come as quite a shock to hear this visitor who claimed the Lord hated and despised their festivals and assemblies and wouldn't accept their offerings. How would we feel if a prophet stood in one of our Sunday gatherings and told us God said we needed to be quiet because he refused to listen to us? Amos said the music wasn't the important thing here; instead, in 5.24: '*let justice roll down like waters, and righteousness like an ever-flowing stream*'! Likewise, in Isaiah 58, we hear God's people complaining that he's not listening to their prayers or noticing that they've fasted. Why? Because they then 'do as they please' and exploit their workers, arguing and fighting (v. 3). Instead, God says he wants them to 'loose the chains of injustice and untie the cords of the yoke, to set the oppressed free', to share their food with those who are hungry, to provide shelter to those in need, and to clothe the naked.

Throughout the Scriptures, we see how important justice is to God; surely, true worship increasingly makes us more like the one we worship? As we focus on God, we gain more of his heart and begin to care more about the things he cares about. And we see through Amos, Isaiah and many other prophets that relationship with God brings responsibilities as well as blessings. Amos wants the Israelites to see the world through a different lens and reshape their responsibilities so that they understand it is not good enough to avoid evil, but they must also seek good; it's not enough to worship when they gather, they must worship as they scatter and look after those in need. As a redeemed people, we are meant to live out our redemption in our lives with others. In other words, our worship leads to action.

Extravagant love overflows through worship into action

In 2012 I went to Eastern Africa with a small team from my church; that trip changed my life. From the moment we arrived and were surrounded by noisy, joyful children who couldn't stop saying thank you that we had come from so far to visit, I knew it would humble me and mark a big shift in my life. There is a real danger in these sorts of mission trips that Westerners picture themselves as the 'saviours' riding on their chargers into Africa with their money and expertise that will solve all the problems. What these beautiful African people possessed was something that money simply cannot buy: a lifestyle where Jesus is at the centre, where the daily distractions of life do not get in the way of a complete dependence on God's loving generosity towards his people. Almost instantaneously, I had a sense of God's voice saying that I needed to watch and listen very carefully. I needed to lose any sense that I was there to teach, rather he was about to teach and train me through these Spirit-filled people what whole-life, whole-self worship was all about. I don't have time here to tell you how God used that trip to heal me and to show me his incredible love in new ways – how he gave me the chance to love and experience compassion beyond my human capability. But I will say he opened within me a desire for justice that would start to shape a new direction in my life.

On my return from Africa, many of my colleagues at work recognized the shift that had taken place in me, and my renewed passion for justice was encouraged by those around me. After taking my son on our annual pantomime trip, Luke and I bounced out of the theatre, singing the silly songs, when we almost tripped over a homeless young man. He looked so desperate, and our mood quickly changed. We spoke to him for a while and picked up some of his story as an ex-soldier. This encounter really made an impact on Luke, and in the weeks that followed, he prayed about it each day in childlike simplicity, 'Dear Lord, please show my mummy what to do!'

A short while later, I arrived in my office one morning to an e-mail asking for volunteers across the bank to help the homeless of Chester. It was then that I got involved in raising funds to support in the rehabilitation and practical help for the 63 people who lived on the streets of my local city. The bank supported us with matched funds and by giving us time off to organize team days so that we could play our part in making a difference in our local community. The volunteer team bonded around this, and their eyes were opened to different challenges. This early work then led to greater opportunities to invest time with these people who were homeless, providing greater care and beginning discussions that would start to address the root cause of the problems they faced. Once again, I was witnessing how when our hearts are open, authentic worship can overflow into action wherever we are, not just when we go overseas, but in the places where God opens the doors in our everyday lives.

Gathered and scattered church worship

Both gathered and scattered worship are equally vital – our worship in church equips us to glorify God on our frontlines. The transition we experience as we are sent as gathered worshippers into the world is such a pivotal moment, when worship turns from adoration towards God and, in the power of the Holy Spirit, to one another, into our scattered lives in the world to which we are sent to act for God's glory.

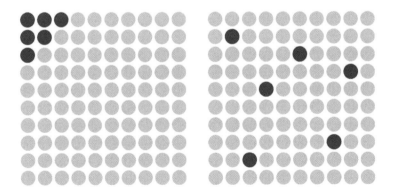

The red dots in the corner of the left-hand side of the picture represent the percentage of people in the UK who worship in a church once a month or more across all denominations and traditions.

The grey dots represent those in our towns, villages or cities who are not engaged with a church. The square to the right-hand side of the picture represents the same people but from the perspective of where they are for most of the week – *scattered* throughout towns, villages, cities and beyond, touching all aspects of life including families, friends and local communities; education, government, sports, healthcare, media, arts and entertainment; and business and commerce. Our reach as Christians is extensive, and our spheres of influence are powerful if intentionally directed in the power of the Holy Spirit to God's glory. We are in touch with so many 'grey dots' as we navigate through life; for many of those people, we may be one of the few Christians they ever encounter.

In each week there are 168 hours. If we have a reasonably healthy sleep pattern, we sleep for around 48 hours, leaving 120 hours. For most people, the maximum number of hours they can dedicate to gathered church activity is 10 hours – for example, worship on a Sunday, small group activity and possibly a commitment to some specific area of ministry; that leaves 110. So, what is happening in the 110 hours when we are not worshipping at church? How do we worship God in these places?

The 6Ms

Up until 2016, I spent most of my life working in the banking industry. I always felt deeply blessed in my career and was fortunate to work with such wonderful people. For 27 years I directed major change transformation programmes, and it was such an exciting vocation. I always felt that I was exactly where God wanted me to be, learning to be a disciple among both the ordinary and extraordinary days of my life as I progressed in my career, then became a wife and a mum and juggled my career and my ministry in my local church alongside ministerial training, first as a Church of England reader and then as a priest – all these joys alongside the more difficult moments of my life as I navigated through suffering and grief.

As I look back over my years as a business leader, I wish that I had really understood then what I know so clearly now. While I knew I was where I was supposed to be and I knew I was a disciple in the places where God placed me, I don't think I realized the true significance of being a Christian in the workplace until my very last day in banking. As people came to visit me to say their goodbyes, people who were uncertain about faith and some who had no faith shared with me the impact it had on them to work with a Christian. There were some big things about walking beside people and showing wisdom, love and compassion during the storms of life; moulding culture in a way that shifted the more ruthless natures of the corporate world to a community with good and loving values; and taking some big risks for my teams speaking up for injustice and against malpractice. And there were some smaller, everyday things about just bringing joy and peace in a stressful environment. I just wish I had realized that God was at work in that place as clearly as he was on a Sunday when I was with my church family.

At LICC we talk about the *6Ms* of *M*odelling godly character, *M*aking good work, *M*inistering grace and love, *M*oulding culture, being a *M*outhpiece for truth and justice and being a *M*essenger of the gospel. Each of the 6Ms enhances another and multiplies fruitfulness on our frontlines when used all together. The 6Ms expand our vision of what it means to be a fruitful Christian in our everyday life.

Modelling godly character is the fruit of the Spirit in action – love, joy, peace, patience, kindness, goodness, faithfulness, gentleness and self-control. When were these qualities particularly required in your life? Or tested? Do people notice something different about your default response to situations? The Fruit of the Holy Spirit sums up nine attributes of a person or community living in accordance with the Holy Spirit (Galatians 5.22–23), where the fruit is contrasted with the works of the flesh which immediately precede it in this chapter of Galatians.

Making good work. The work that we do matters in and of itself. The way we do our work is important, whatever the context, whether as a parent, in our studies, in our paid work or volunteering. Our attitude to our work, the way we give our best, the excellence we work for, suggests our attitude to life and the values and beliefs that underpin why we work the way we do. Giving our absolute best is fundamental, but what does it mean to make good work with God? Working with a consciousness that we work for the Lord, in the Spirit, to his glory means producing work that is 'good' beyond simply human effort. 'Whatever you do, work at it with all your heart, as working for the Lord, not for human masters' (Colossians 3.23).

Ministering grace and love. Here the attitudes of the heart are brought to bear in specific situations. How do you love someone who is feeling unwell or upset, someone who is particularly difficult? And it is not just the more superficial actions; really loving someone can be hard. How do you minister grace and love in a redundancy situation when you are the person pulling the trigger? Or when a colleague at work is not pulling his or her weight? Or when someone in your family does something to hurt you? Or a friend lets you down when you really needed help? In the way that Christ has forgiven us for our imperfections and sins, so must we find in us the grace to minister love towards others, 'For it is by grace you have been saved, through faith – and this is not from yourselves, it is the gift of God – not by works, so that no one can boast. For we are God's handiwork, created in Christ Jesus to do good works, which God prepared in advance for us to do' (Ephesians 2.8–10).

Mould culture. If culture is 'the way we do things round here', how do we influence the way things are done in our homes, in our church, in our workplace and among our friends? First, we must be aware of the values behind the actions, attitudes and norms of our front-line places. How could our Christian values lead to different practice, to different outcomes, to renewed cultures in all those places? Remember we can affect culture even if we are not in a position of power or authority; sometimes it requires us to graciously name what is wrong and what needs to change.

Be a Mouthpiece for truth and justice. There will be times when being a Christian in the variety of contexts that represent our frontlines means speaking up against things that are unfair, unhealthy or untruthful and speaking for things that are true and just and good. This can be for our own benefit but is perhaps more pertinent when we are speaking up on someone else's behalf and there is a risk involved in our putting our head above the parapet. 'Do nothing from selfish ambition or conceit, but in humility regard others as better than yourselves' (Philippians 2.3). We cannot relieve God's disappointment in our lack of action for justice through singing songs and offering prayers when we gather to worship. We may give thanks for all that is good in life, we may praise God for his goodness and mercy, we may confess what we and others have done wrong, and perhaps we lament for the pain and difficulty we and others are experiencing. Yet if we do not carry with us our Christian responsibility to ensure justice is done, how do we present ourselves before God as we worship? Worship is not for compensating for the injustice that we perpetrate in our gathered or scattered lives; rather it is for presenting our whole life and whole self before God.

Be a Messenger for the Gospel. There are times when people want to hear your story and what values and beliefs underpin your life, and you will tell them about Jesus and the difference he has made to you. We each have a unique story and a testimony that is always developing – especially if we are truly, authentically and intentionally living out our faith. Have you had an opportunity to share the message of Jesus with somebody recently? Are you prepared? 'But in your hearts sanctify Christ as Lord. Always be ready to make your defence to anyone who demands from you an accounting for the hope that is in you' (1 Peter 3.15). Are you intentional in your relationships and committed to praying for them?

Let me tell you about Ed. Ed wants to be more open about his faith within his workplace, an IT company. Ed describes the culture of where he works as, 'It's the kind of place where the only sign that you're doing a great job is that nobody has shouted at you that day.' Like many of us might in a place like that, Ed kept his faith quiet and separate. His love for God was deepening, his character was changing and his involvement with church was growing, but when Monday morning rolled around, Ed's own faith was compartmentalized away from the gathered worship he had enjoyed on Sunday. Then one day, Ed decided he would be more open at work about his Christian faith. First 'a few safe people', but it wasn't long before he had talked to ten of his colleagues about Jesus. He didn't have to force the issue nor did he have to say a lot. So when Ed was asked 'What did you get up to over the weekend?' by one colleague, as well as mentioning family time, jobs done and films watched, Ed also mentioned that he had led the children's work at church.

While a few colleagues make jokes about Ed being a Christian, most of them have been surprisingly accepting. His great fears about going public were not confirmed. This brave but simple change of posture has opened a whole new world of opportunities. Lots of his colleagues now confide in him in ways that they never did before. One colleague shared with him how his wife had a very serious health problem and that he was desperately worried about her. Ed offered to pray, and the colleague accepted, and in time, thanks to God, the wife of this colleague got completely better. Your frontline might not be like Ed's. You might not be like Ed, and being more open on your frontline might cause you more problems than it did for him. But when we stop treating our faith like a secret to be kept and we share the light of Christ for all to glimpse God's beauty and colour within us, we might find ourselves being pleasantly surprised when we adopt a posture of openness.

We, God's people, are created in his likeness

God has always longed for us, his people, to live in complete union with him, to imitate him, through Christ and in the power of the Spirit. We, the Church, are the body of people who God created in his likeness and redeemed, and when we come together in worship and praise of him, he listens to all that makes us cry out. Our worship, if it is authentic, will be pleasing to God, and it will energize, inspire and equip us for his purposes for us in every aspect of our life. In it, we will be renewed in the love of Christ, a love that will create in us a compassion beyond our own strength, that will overflow and have an impact on the lives of others in our everyday lives, whatever we do, wherever we are, all of the time.

As we give ourselves fully to Christ in all our life, we will be filled with passionate hearts that not only re-shape the direction of our own lives, but also those whose lives we touch. God opens the doors for us to make a difference in our everyday lives, showing us how to live fruitful lives where we can change the world through the fruits of the Spirit that we possess. Fruits of love, joy, peace, patience, kindness, goodness, faithfulness, gentleness and self-control. As we are unleashed and sent out into our scattered lives praying '*your* kingdom come', may we continually be reminded that we are called to model God's character; every work we do, no matter how menial, should be to the glory of God; Jesus calls us to minister grace and love in his name and to reshape and remould culture to one that exemplifies the nature of Christ. We need to remember that justice is God's cause, a cause we join in with if we are willing to restore the world back to its original purpose. And each of us is called to be ready to proclaim the gospel to anyone who demands from us an accounting for the hope that is in each of us. I wonder where God might be nudging you to make a difference in your everyday life ...

Further resources for digging deeper

Visit

Mark Greene – *Fruitfulness on the Frontline: Making a Difference Wherever You Are*

Sam and Sara Hargreaves – *Whole Life Worship: Empowering Disciples for the Frontline*

Joe Warton – *Whole Life Worship Study Guide*

Neil Hudson – *Imagine Church: Releasing Whole Life Disciples*

Neil Hudson – *Scattered and Gathered: Equipping Disciples for the Frontline*

Mark Greene – *The Great Divide*

Mike Pilavachi – *For the Audience of One: Worshipping the One and Only in Everything You Do*

Louie Giglio – *The Air I Breathe: Worship as a Way of Life*

John Piper – *Let the Nations Be Glad*

Glenn Packiam – *Blessed Broken Given: How Your Story Becomes Sacred in the Hands of Jesus*

Part 3

WHAT HAPPENS WHEN WE WORSHIP?

Worship is for God; that is agreed. But worshipping God also seems to benefit us! Pope Pius X, writing on church music at the beginning of the twentieth century, said that worship is for 'the glorification of God and the sanctification of humanity'. In other words, worship not only gives glory to God but also acts to transform us. Worship is God's gift to us to enable us to fulfil our calling and to be his representatives, his *image* on earth. In fact, by fulfilling our calling, we *are* glorifying God! We can confidently say that worship is for our own good – that 'the glory of God is a human being fully alive' (St Irenaeus). In Part 3 we explore this idea with three chapters on surrender, intimacy and the power of praise.

We begin by exploring the crucial theme of intimacy in worship. Worship enables and encourages an openness in our hearts to the heart of God. Kees Kraayenoord shares his own story of vulnerability before God and encourages us to do the same: 'It takes the real you to step into intimacy with the Father. Not the "spiritual you", the "you" you want people to believe you are.' He continues by encouraging us to walk closely with God and take up the gift of true relationship that worship provides – God doesn't want employees but friends who share his heart.

Chapter 9 opens with the announcement from Noel Robinson that 'praise is a weapon!'

We learn that worship is not like any other earthly power, though. It is a cross-shaped posture that releases faith in the things unseen rather than merely living by fear of what we can see. He writes, 'It's a weapon that God has given us, not to wreck destruction but to bring breakthrough in difficult times.' Noel shares deeply from his own life and describes how it is possible to turn petition into praise, no matter what the circumstance we face. He reminds us too that children model this kind of faith, this simple-hearted praise: 'Through the praise of children and infants you have established a stronghold against your enemies, to silence the foe and the avenger' (Ps 8.2).

The final chapter in this section looks at how worship invites and enables our surrender to God. Opening with the fascinating story of the writer of the famous hymn 'I Surrender All', Doug Williams explores the hard truth that 'it is much easier to sing about submission than it is to actually do it!' By journeying through some of the biblical theology and explaining why surrender goes against our fallen nature, Doug goes on to encourage us in the way of Jesus who surrendered all to the will of the Father: 'The principle of surrender is central to the Christian concept of worship.'

As you read through this section, be praying for God to highlight one or two key things to apply in your own life. Perhaps it will be a renewal of your sense of intimacy with him, or perhaps you need to lay down some things, hopes or dreams that have become idols and surrender afresh to the Lord. Perhaps you will need to stand up and just declare praise over whatever situation you are facing. Whatever it is, you are not on your own – the Holy Spirit is with you to empower you to grow as a worshipper and to become more like Jesus.

DR NICK DRAKE

8

Worship and intimacy

KEES KRAAYENOORD

Kees is a Dutch worship leader who planted Mozaiek0318 church with his wife, Nicole, in 2013. He has been leading worship and writing songs for around 30 years and was instrumental in setting up Worship Central Netherlands, with the aim of training and equipping worship leaders, musicians and worshippers.

When I was younger, so much younger than today, I had only one desire. If that sounds very holy and biblical, let me point out that my one desire wasn't to 'live in the house of the Lord', as David writes in Psalm 27. No, I wanted to be a rock star. That was all I wanted. Even as a young kid, I used a tennis racket for a guitar, borrowed my brother's headphones and, while others played with cars or a football, I played 'rock and roll singer' in my bedroom. That dream didn't die when I became a Christian at the age of 15. I still wanted to sing, perform and stir people's hearts with my voice but now as a worship leader.

Our little church was discovering the power of praise and worship, and by the age of 17, my biggest hero was Graham Kendrick. I wanted to be like him, sing like him and even look like him. It's funny now, but I believed that God had given me a voice and a song to lead others into his presence. However, in my teenage ambition, I was at times more excited about the act of worship than the heart of worship. Perhaps I was a bit more into the music than excited about intimacy with God.

One Sunday morning, I was scheduled to play piano in church. I wasn't leading worship, but I did have a microphone at the piano to sing harmonies. I was 30 feet from stardom but fulfilled that BV role with quite some energy and enthusiasm. Perhaps a bit too much energy and enthusiasm . . . A few minutes before the service began, I saw one of the elders of our church, who was also a worship leader, heading towards me. It turned out he had been assigned by his fellow leaders to bring me some bad news. He leaned forward and said, 'Kees, I forgot to drop by or call you earlier, but as elders we have decided that you are not allowed to sing here for a while.'

Was this a bad joke? My fingers stopped in mid-air over the keys as I stammered, 'Why not?'

'Well, we got letters, you see. It seems that there are some here who feel that your voice and the way you sing are, quite frankly, very annoying. Complaints have been received about you. Angry letters. People have a hard time worshipping because of . . . you. So, for the time being, you are not allowed to sing here. I hope you understand.'

Before I could say a word, he took my microphone, unplugged it from the cord, and walked away with it. Dazed, I stared at the empty microphone holder in which a small cable dangled gently back and forth. My head didn't know what to think and my heart didn't know what to feel and there was little time to figure that out, because the service had started as if *nothing was wrong*! But everything was wrong. And, as though heaven was playing a joke on me, one of the songs that morning (a Graham Kendrick song, no less) said, 'O Lord, Your tenderness, melting all my bitterness'. For me, there was not a lot of 'melting bitterness' taking place. I felt so misunderstood, hurt and angry.

After the service, I gathered my family and friends and told them what 'those elders' had done to me. I shared my anger. They all agreed, sharing some of their frustrations, saying that this wasn't a very pastoral thing to do. They felt sorry for me . . . for a while. But when someone tried to change the subject, I quickly made sure that it came back round to how I had been wronged. I talked about it with everyone I could, and I kept talking about it to anyone who would listen. Everyone, that is, except God.

At the end of that crazy Sunday, I came home to an empty house. For the first time since that morning, I was completely on my own. I was alone, and that's exactly where God was waiting for me. His still small voice spoke loud and clear in my heart:

'Is it right that you are so angry?'

'Yes, God, it is! Do you know what they did to me?'

'Yes, I know. And I also know they hurt you deeply by taking your microphone away.'

'You can say that again. Thanks for understanding. This isn't right, is it?'

'But son, what do you want?'

'I just want to sing, Lord. I want to sing for you! Why don't they get that?'

'Well, if that's what you want – I'm here! If you want to sing for me, sing for me!'

Immediately, my anger gave way to tears. I broke down as I understood for the first time in my life that I didn't need a church or a group of people to be able to sing to God. I didn't need a stage or a microphone. My 17-year-old ambitious, wannabe worship leader heart started to understand that I only needed God and his precious presence. God just wanted to be with me, no microphone required.

I picked up my guitar and said, 'Father, this worship concert is for you and you alone!' And I *sang*! I sang like my life depended on it. I played the guitar and danced around my room. My bedroom was the platform, and God's angels were my church. I'd like to believe they sang along – at least I didn't get any complaints from the heavenly choir that I was singing with too much energy or enthusiasm. That night, the Father sang his song of love over my life, and I sang with him. I returned my song of worship to him. The elders of my church may have taken my microphone, but they could never take my voice. And my voice was for none other than the one who had given me my voice.

That night of worship in my bedroom was one of the rawest and most intimate moments of worship of my life. Why? It was all about being real and completely honest. Honesty and intimacy go really well together. They belong to each other.

Real love

It takes the real you to step into intimacy with the Father. Not the 'spiritual you', the 'you' you'd like to be, or the 'you' you want people to believe you are. There is beauty in all of us but it's often hidden under a pile of hurt, sin, mistakes and ways we've been badly treated. But we are still created in God's image. His fingerprints are all over us and over *all* of us! And let's remember God didn't create us because he was alone or to have people to remind him how great he us. No, he didn't have to create us; he *wanted* to. God was not alone. God was and is Father, Son and Holy Spirit. The early Desert fathers called it Perichoresis, the dance of the Trinity.[1] God is a dancing God, three in one. He is a holy, loving, passionate communion. The Father loves the Son. The Son loves the Father. The Holy Spirit loves the Father, and so on. The Father shouts: This is my Son in whom I am well pleased. The Son sings: This is my Father whom I love and serve. And the Holy Spirit is the ultimate worship leader, stirring our hearts, pouring out passion, and setting the church on fire to worship and praise the Father and Son like there's no tomorrow.

So that's why we were created. For love. For friendship. For intimacy. God created Adam and Eve, not just to have some employees to look after his garden, but so he could walk with them, talk with them, and share his heart with them.

---

1   *Perichoresis* (from Greek: περιχώρησις *perikhōrēsis*, "rotation") is a term referring to the relationship of the three persons of the triune God (Father, Son, and Holy Spirit) to one another.

When intimacy gets lost

Much ink has been expended writing about what we call 'the fall' – Adam and Eve's disobedience. You've heard the story: the tree, the fruit, the snake, the heartache, the terrible loss. But have you thought about the fact that after Adam and Eve stepped away from God, God didn't say, 'What have you done?' Or even, 'What were you thinking?' He cried, 'Where *are* you?' Let that sink in for a moment. God didn't blame them. He missed them. He was searching for them. When something valuable gets lost, you search for it. And God just lost a friendship. His missed his intimate friends, Adam and Eve, and – in them – you and me. 'Where are you?' God cried in the garden and continues to cry now. 'My son, my daughter, where are you? I miss you.'

I dare you to believe that God loves you so much that he actually wants to spend time with you like he did with Adam and Eve. The garden of Eden was perhaps the first temple in that it was a meeting place for humankind and God. A 'heaven meets earth' reality. If that's true, you could say that the tabernacle of Moses in the book of Exodus is an attempt to go back to how things were. An attempt to restore the intimacy which got lost.

After the exodus, after years of slavery in Egypt, God led his people into the desert. On their way to the Promised Land, God spoke to Moses, saying, 'The people must make a sacred tent for me, so that I may live among them' (Ex. 25.8). It wasn't just the people who were homesick. God still wanted to be with and hang with his friends. It seems that the dance isn't over. After the tent was finished, God showed up in all of his glory. That must have been quite a show! Scripture says that Moses couldn't even enter the tent because of God's majesty filling the place. There was only room for one in this tent. There was even a curtain to block the way to the holy and secret place. This was an attempt to go back to how things were in the garden, but it doesn't come close to the real and intimate friendship there once was.

Years later, in the promised land, Solomon, David's boy, built God a temple. Of course, David, the worshipper-king, had a thirst and hunger for God's presence like we've never seen before. David was a worshipper, and he wanted to build God a real house, a meeting place for God to dwell and for man to worship. But, again, it didn't heal the wound and restore what was lost. God's glory fell, and once more the people had a hard time entering the place because of it. Imagine that after all the blood, sweat and tears, after all the years of hard work, the blisters, the splinters in their hands, after all the money and gold people invested, you hear the king say, 'But will God indeed dwell on the earth? Behold, heaven and the highest heaven cannot contain you; how much less this house that I have built!' (1 Kings 8.27). I can hear the foreman ask Solomon, Now, *why* did we built this place again?

It's all for intimacy, isn't it? Friendship between God and humankind. A meeting place for the Creator and the created one. But this place too has a curtain so thick that even the strongest man on earth couldn't tear it apart. The relationship is broken, and even though we call the tabernacle and temple 'the house of God', it doesn't seem to heal the wounds. It doesn't fix the intimate relationship of love we have been created for. We're still homesick. Intimacy is still lost.

Is there hope? How can we ever come close? Where do we go from here?

We turn to Jesus!

Or, more accurately, in Jesus, God turned to us. For this is what John, the evangelist, says in his first chapter: 'And the Word (Jesus) became flesh and dwelt among us, and we have seen his glory, glory as of the only Son from the Father, full of grace and truth' (John 1.14).

In the Greek, the word for 'dwell' is 'pitching a tent'. It doesn't take a scholar to see what John is doing here. He's pointing back to the tabernacle and temple, the heaven and earth reality, where glory meets dirt. But this time, the meeting place isn't a tent or building; it's flesh and blood. This temple lives. This temple has a name. And his name is Jesus. John even speaks of 'glory'. Remember when God's glory filled the tabernacle and temple? Now the Son shows up in all of his glory!

I love how Eugene Peterson puts it in *The Message*: 'The Word became flesh and blood, and moved into the neighborhood. We saw the glory with our own eyes, the one-of-a-kind glory, like Father, like Son. Generous inside and out, true from start to finish' (John 1.4).

And there's more! Remember God saying to Moses, 'No man can see me and live'? God is changing things around. Let the healing begin. For now, in Jesus, we see God for who he really is. We are staring into the face of God, looking in the eyes of love . . . and we live!

John ends this passage stronger than we could ever dream of: 'No one has ever seen God, not so much as a glimpse. This one-of-a-kind God-Expression, who exists at the very heart of the Father, has made him plain as day. Thunder in the Desert' (John 1.18, MSG).

'At the very heart of the Father'! In Dutch (my language) and also in the Greek, it says that this Jesus, '*being in or resting at the bosom of the Father*', Jesus has made the Father known. It doesn't get more intimate than this. Do you see yourself at the bosom of the Father? In Jesus, you can! In him, all lives can be restored. In him, we can be friends again. In him, God is asking us to dance once again. Jesus came to restore and heal what was broken. Intimacy can be restored. The door is open.

Let's jump to the end of Jesus's life. The moment he cries, 'It is done', that curtain so thick no one could tear is torn! From top to bottom. The Father himself tears it in two, inviting us to come closer, to step into the holy place. God's children are welcomed home to the bosom of Abba. The writer of the book of Hebrews says it like this:

So, friends, we can now - without hesitation - walk right up to God, into 'the Holy Place.' Jesus has cleared the way by the blood of his sacrifice, acting as our priest before God. The 'curtain' into God's presence is his body. So let's do it – full of belief, confident that we're presentable inside and out. (Hebrews 10.19, MSG)

Through Jesus's death, we can go through the curtain and into the most holy and intimate place.

As a worship leader, while leading God's people, my mind is often full. Though I'm presenting my heart to the one we worship, there's a lot of stuff going on in my head at the same time. I'm asking important questions, such as, 'God, is this the right direction?' Or 'Is there something you want to say or do right now?' I also have less spiritual questions too, like, 'Do I need to tune my guitar again?' Or 'Will the team remember this musical break we rehearsed?' Now and then, there's no room for questions. Sometimes God's presence is there in such a tangible and powerful way the only response is awe, silence or even tears. I remember one time leading a song called 'Hosanna'. In the bridge we sang, 'Break my heart with what breaks yours.' I can't explain what happened, but it was like God's glory came down. His presence was, as some might say, thick! We went beyond the song, beyond the veil. What we prayed and sang about happened. God started to break our hearts. And instead of going to the chorus, like we rehearsed, we stayed there for a while. We couldn't just move on. Our worship became a time of rededication, of sacrifice, of surrender. People started to cry and, instead of singing, we started praying. I remember one of our prayer team lying on the floor, banging, crying, weeping, shouting. And he wasn't the only one. My microphone was forgotten; I had to lay down my guitar so I could lie on the floor, face down. God's presence touched us and broke our hearts with what breaks his heart. It was a moment where worship and intercession came together. It was not about the songs any more, but all about his will, his heart, his desire. These moments are special, because they're life-changing!

Overflowing love

We see one of the most beautiful examples of intimate worship in the Bible in Luke 7.36–50, where a woman pours a jar of perfume over Jesus's feet, weeping, wiping his feet with her hair and kissing them. There is a lot we don't know about this woman. How did she get into Simon's house in the first place? When did she and Jesus meet for the first time? What happened when they met? We don't know the answers to these questions, but her meeting with Jesus must have been extraordinary. She must have felt his love. She must have experienced forgiveness. She must have felt heaven's acceptance. We can only guess. Luke, the evangelist, doesn't even share her name with us.[2] He just shares her *reputation* with us. She is 'the woman known in the city as a sinner'. She is known for being the town's harlot. But Jesus changed her life. He opened the door to the Father, welcoming her into God's secret place. We don't know when or where. We only know that this woman, known for being a sinner, is about to receive a *new* reputation. The one who was known for her sin is now the one we know for her sacrifice, for her love, for her worship. Luke says that she came with a bottle of expensive perfume and stood at Jesus's feet, weeping. 'Raining tears on his feet', as *The Message* puts it. She even let down her hair and dried his feet. Perhaps that doesn't seem shocking to you, but in first-century Middle Eastern culture, that was not the done thing. She did it anyway. She didn't do it in private, but in front of everyone. Of course, Simon condemned the scene, the woman, and even Jesus. And, to make it even worse, she started to kiss the feet of Jesus and anointed them with the perfume she brought.

The intimacy is evident. She loved Jesus. She worshipped him. It seems that she didn't even mind what the others were thinking. This

---

2   In the other gospels there are similar stories of a woman anointing Jesus's feet. In John's version, the woman is Mary, sister of Martha. We can't be sure, though, whether this is just another angle of the same story, or a different one.

was her chance to return all the love that was given to her. She seized the moment. It may look inappropriate, but it isn't. There is nothing more appropriate than returning God's love with our kisses, our intimacy, our worship.

Worship and intimacy are not just for behind closed doors. 'There's a time for everything', according to the writer of Ecclesiastes. Yes, there is a time to close the door behind you and meet the Father alone, as Graham wrote about in Chapter 5. That one night in my bedroom, when I had come home from church angry and disappointed, I needed one of those 'secret' moments. But at other times, we need to be a bit bolder, not keep our love for Jesus quiet, and find that we can have intimacy with Jesus even in a crowded room. Some might judge us for being too noisy, too bold, too free or too unpolished. But remember the woman anointing Jesus's feet. She let down her hair and kissed Jesus's feet . . . *in public*. Remember her and feel encouraged to go where she goes and do what she does. Sometimes we need to celebrate in public what we received in private.

I remember one night at a worship conference when I was in my twenties, a pastor got on stage right after the time of sung worship. The band was still playing softly. With a Scottish accent, he said: 'Jesus, we want you to know tonight that we are totally, totally, totally, totally in love with you. Lord, we could kiss you right now.' And that's what he started to do. I kid you not. He started to make kissing sounds in the microphone. Encouraged by this, some people around me some started to make kissing sounds as well. I thought they'd all gone completely mad! I felt like the only normal person in the room. I remember thinking to myself: 'God, what are these crazy people doing?' Then, a still small voice in my heart said, 'These crazy people know they've been found by my crazy love, and they are just crazy about me. How about you?'

The next moment I was throwing hand kisses to the sky. I really went for it. I felt liberated! I started to laugh, and I'm sure Jesus was laughing too. It was like he was saying, 'Don't care about what others think. It's just you and me – and I love to be kissed by you.'

Now, I'm not suggesting that we make this a regular part of our worship services! I know how crazy it sounds, and I'd never done it before and I've never done it since. Don't be put off; making kissing noises isn't the formula to intimacy with Jesus! My point is that there are times to go a little further than before, to celebrate in public what God gave us in private. No matter what others are thinking.

Why? Because I believe that when we show intimacy, we will grow in intimacy too. My wife, Nicole, and I love to walk, and when we do, we often hold hands. It's not just a sign of our love; it actually builds our love too. I believe that to be true of public worship and intimacy. On one hand, our public worship is the result of intimacy and honesty, but as we learn to show it and to share it with others, we also grow more intimacy.

God loves you. He loves you, no matter your reputation. No matter what people call you, he calls you his friend. He wants to be with you. He enjoys being kissed by you. He loves to kiss you. Really! I'm not making this up. I'm not being soft or sentimental. This is Jesus talking about the prodigal son: 'He was still a long way from home when his father saw him; his heart was filled with pity, and he ran, threw his arms around his son, and kissed him[3].'

That's the Father's heart for you and me today. Come a little closer. We're welcome. We're loved. Just as we are.

Further resources for digging deeper

Tim Hughes – *Here I Am to Worship*
Andy Park – *To Know You More*
Marva J. Dawn – *A Royal Waste of Time*
Darlene Zschech – *Extravagant Worship*

---

3   Luke 15:20 Good News Translation

9

Power and praise

NOEL ROBINSON

Noel is an international worship leader, music pastor, songwriter and producer, and one of the pioneers of the British Gospel sound. He has been involved in worship ministry for over 20 years, working with many ministries and starting his own event called Renewal Worship Encounters. Noel's heart is to see unity across the body of Christ and he aims to carry a message of revival, reformation and restoration to the Church and world.

Praise is a weapon. It's a weapon that God has given us, not to wreak destruction but to bring breakthrough in difficult times. Because we don't just praise when life is going well and our thanksgiving trips off our tongue with no conscious thought from us. Praise can be employed in the darkest of times, reminding us of who God is, declaring the truth of his goodness no matter what our circumstances, and connecting us to his presence and his power in a life-changing way. It's not about living in cloud cuckoo land where we blithely say, 'I am so blessed' and pretend everything is perfect. This is about having a joy in the Lord that isn't determined by external factors.

Let's look at the biblical context for the word 'praise'.

King David was chosen by God to carry the leadership of his generation and was in a position to reform 'praise'. We are told that David, *the king*, responded to God by dancing in a way so undignified it was not befitting to his position! The people watching saw a person respond to the presence of God with all his might and strength.

Perhaps David did not discover this exuberant expression of praise while he was in the palace, but rather in the fields and valleys as he had looked after his father's sheep. He had experienced the incredible hand of God in battle, and yet he had developed an insight into who God was in all that he could see in nature. He knew that God was with him, and to praise him was a key to God's abiding presence.

If we look at the Psalms – known as Israel's songbook, that includes many written by David – we learn about the power of praise. A number of different Hebrew words are used throughout the psalms which have been translated as 'praise'. As Lou discussed in her chapter, there are words that mean to boast or rave, to make music and song, to extend our hands, to shout and more.

One key verse which establishes the power of praise is Psalms 8.2. I love how the King James version translates it: 'Out of the mouth of babes and sucklings hast thou ordained strength because of thine enemies, that thou mightest still the enemy and the avenger.' With these words, David reminds us that God has ordained an earthly response that silences the enemy. God has established earthly expressions and intentions – declarations of praise – that have an impact on spiritual dimensions around your life. He has given your praise ability, power and spiritual authority to stop the working of the enemy of your soul.

David's revelation of praise shows us how to engage with the Spirit of God in our lives. We also see it vividly in the New Testament.

Praise in prison

We see the power of this at work in Acts 16 when Paul and Silas were in prison. They had been imprisoned, 'severely flogged' and had their feet put into stocks. Despite these challenging circumstances, they were praying and singing songs to God in the middle of the night. It's a natural human reaction to pray to God when you're in a difficult position, but what Paul and Silas did was allow that prayer to turn into praise. When we allow God to move us from petition to praise, we enter the realm of breakthrough.

That night, as Paul and Silas praised, God's presence came, breaking into the prison and causing the earth to quake. The chains that were holding Paul and Silas began to break. Not only that, but those around them were set free too. Your praise can release your family, friends, colleagues and others who have been captured. This is the power of a confession of praise! For the prisoners, they didn't even have to run away and leave the jail; they were freed right where they stood. In the same way, when we're going through difficult times, praise may not change our physical and emotional circumstances, but it can free us in our hearts. Praise changes the atmosphere of prisons – physical and otherwise!

I wonder if many of the situations in which we have found ourselves would have turned out if we had turned our petition to praise? I'm not intending to negate our human experience and our fears, but I truly believe that praise allows us to superimpose God's culture and purpose onto our lives.

I myself have attested to the power of praise, having gone through the traumatic breakdown of a close personal relationship. It tore my very inner being, and I was truly broken by it. There were layers of pain and deception around the breakdown that rocked me to my core. I felt so alone because I didn't know how to confide in anyone, desperate as I was to protect everyone involved. I struggled to truly understand my feelings, and when I saw a counsellor, he said he couldn't help me because I couldn't articulate enough of what had happened for him to help me work through it. I had days of feeling numb and empty, followed by ones where I could do nothing but weep. My body started to suffer, and I lost so much weight that when people saw me for the first time in a while, they thought I had been ravaged by cancer.

While I didn't know how to speak about what I was going through, I began to try and sing. I wrote a song that said, 'You are my healer in times of trouble, when you show up strong, I overcome.' I remember writing that on a day where I had no idea if I would ever overcome the crippling pain, as it seemed like it would never end. And as I began to call on name of the Lord, my petition turned to praise. I proclaimed truths, not about where I was at the time, but about where God's word said I could be. I realized the true power of my praise, of adoring God and worshipping him. There was no miraculous single moment like there was for Paul and Silas in their physical chains but, over time, as I praised, God healed my broken heart and restored my soul.

We see praise precede breakthrough in the story of Jonah too. Many of us know that Jonah was thrown overboard and swallowed by a big fish, but how much have we really thought about his circumstances in connection with our lives? Imagine the utter darkness of being in the belly of a fish. A fish that's big enough to swallow a man whole is a *big* fish, and big fish don't live in shallow water but out in the depths of the ocean. Imagine the pressure of the weight of the water. Imagine being surrounded by everything else the fish had gulped down, the stench of rotting fish filling your nostrils. Knowing your own disobedience and mistakes had led you there. I would guarantee none of us has been in that exact situation, but I'm sure most of us know what pressure feels like. We can testify to times when we've felt like we're surrounded by darkness, times when we feel like life stinks. We've felt trapped, surrounded by death and decay. Hope slips away. Our sins and errors weigh heavily on our shoulders. We feel abandoned and heartbroken, almost to the point of welcoming death.

What did Jonah do in that place? He began to pray and offer up thanksgiving (Jonah 2.9). He didn't wait till life was back on track and he was safely on dry land, clean and out of danger; he praised God in that bleak place. As he did so, the fish spat him out, and he was free.

That's one of the reasons we should praise even when we don't feel like it. True praise is not determined by how we feel. It's not a case of saying, 'I don't feel like praising so I won't.' We should praise God in all seasons. Praising in the dark places, like Jonah, Paul and Silas, doesn't mean we're saying our circumstances are great; we are just saying that God is greater. How do we praise in hard times? We build up the habit of being grateful in our everyday lives.

Your default setting

What is your default setting? For Job, it was praise. We read that he was the wealthiest man in the world, owning seven thousand sheep, three thousand camels, five hundred yoke of oxen, land. He had many servants, and each of his ten children had their own house. His default every morning was to offer a sacrifice to God for each of his children just in case they had sinned. This was an act of worship. When Job heard he'd lost his cattle, his servants and then his children on the same day, he didn't deny his humanity. He tore his robe and shaved his head as was the culture of the day, but then in the next breath he bowed to the ground in worship. That incredible act was no doubt a result of the years he'd spent practicing worship and gratitude each day.

I saw this lived out in my dad when he lost his leg due to diabetes. I got the call that he was in a Jamaican hospital when I was working in the Bahamas, so fortunately it didn't take me too long to get to him. I found him in his hospital bed and saw that they'd had to take his leg off from beneath his knee. All my life, my dad had been my hero; he was an incredibly active man, and it was agonizing to see him in so much pain. Yet every time a wave of pain hit him, he would call out, 'Praise God, hallelujah!'

'Are you crazy?' I asked. 'Don't you feel angry?' I couldn't understand how he could be saying hallelujah when he was in so much pain.

He kept saying, 'Don't worry, I'm still alive. God is good.'

My dad had spent years praising God, so he could ascribe goodness to God even when his world had just changed so dramatically.

He modelled the ability to thank God always, no matter what. He didn't deny his circumstances or his pain; he just chose to speak out the truth of God's goodness, even in those difficult days.

We'll probably all have times when we praise God, believing in a miracle, and then feel that he hasn't delivered us as we'd have liked. The breakthrough hasn't come. Faith says, we praise him regardless. In 2 Samuel 12.20, we read how King David prayed and fasted for his sick son to live. When he died, David 'got up from the floor, washed himself, put lotions on, and changed his clothes. Then he went into the LORD's house to worship.' God is worthy of our praise no matter the outcome of our prayers. He is all he says he is, and our praise of him is important. I can praise God for being my healer because he healed my overactive thyroid and he restored my heart, but I'll also praise him for the things I haven't yet seen. I will praise him for the things the Bible tells me to be true even before I see them. Even in our darkest times, when we 'walk through the valley of the shadow of death' (Psalm 23.4), he is with us. We can always praise him for his love and care for us, for his presence in our lives, even when we're struggling to see it or feel it. The Bible tells us that, without faith, it is impossible to please God. Praise engages our faith. We praise the God of deliverance even though we're not delivered; we praise the God who provides, even if we're walking in lack; we praise the God who heals, even when we're sick.

But as I said at the start, praising God doesn't mean we don't acknowledge the painful circumstances of our lives. In fact, one of the most profound things captured in Scripture is lament. If you're not familiar with the term, it means to express your sadness, regret or disappointment about something. There are more psalms of lament than any other type of psalm, and this shows us how important it was for God that we see these emotions and have permission to express our own sorrow. God doesn't need us to say everything is okay when it isn't; he wants us to have the freedom to be honest in all seasons of life. David's ability to tell his story with authenticity – letting us in on the highs and lows of his emotions – really captures a picture of his humanity. Life can be painful and confusing and we need to make space in our worship and prayer to reflect that. The psalms of lament show us the depth of human emotion, crying out questions like, 'Where are you God? Have you forgotten me?' Yet the vast majority end with praise. David doesn't get stuck in his lament; he is honest about his struggles but then calls to mind God's goodness, and he finds a reason to praise.

Revelation

The more we, like David, focus on God's goodness, the quicker we will be to praise. The more we know him, the faster those words will fall from our tongues. If you have a nice meal that you rave about, you can only praise it because you experienced it. If you drive a car and you love it, you're praising that car's functions because you've tried it. When we praise God, it is a response to the revelation of how good he is. When you value something, you can't help but speak about it.

Romans 10.9–10 says, 'If you declare with your mouth, "Jesus is Lord," and believe in your heart that God raised him from the dead, you will be saved. For it is with your heart that you believe and are justified, and it is with your mouth that you profess your faith and are saved.' We understand here that words carry their power by what we believe in our hearts. Anyone can say the words 'Jesus is Lord', but you have to believe them in your heart for it to carry the power of salvation. Those words are birthed in revelation of who God is; without that, they are empty.

When our hearts are connected to the revelation of who Jesus is, there's a power in our mouths that doesn't come from the words themselves. In Psalm 4, as he brought the Ark of the Covenant to Mount Zion, King David said, 'O clap your hands, all ye people; shout unto God with the voice of triumph.' We can clap our hands or shout, but when we do it with the 'voice of triumph', with the knowledge of God's power and goodness, there is a new power in those actions. This is part of the Holy Spirit's role, as Nick explores in Chapter 4.

Often we have nullified the place of spiritual warfare. The enemy has tried to hinder the thanksgiving in our heart and keep us focused on what we don't have rather than who God is and all he has done for us. He tries to get us to focus on the bad things in our lives, to be jealous of those who have more than we do, rather than focusing on all the good gifts God has given us.

I know I sometimes struggle to find the words when I'm feeling emotionally exhausted. Then I come back to the Bible and praise him with the words I find there. I will say, 'God you are my strength,' even when I feel weak, 'God you are my peace,' even when I don't feel peaceful. I choose to continue to speak about God's goodness, knowing it is real and knowing I can draw on the truth of his words to lead me to him.

One thing that always helps is reflecting on God's character and asking him for fresh revelation of who he is. Here are just some of his names and attributes; I'd encourage you to spend some time studying others whenever you need to focus again on how good God is.

- Abba – God is our Father and wants intimate relationship with us.
- Creator – God made the world and everything in it.
- Deliverer – This was a name David favoured, probably as he saw God deliver him from so many enemies. Though we won't see God deliver us from every bad situation on earth, he has provided the ultimate deliverance for us in his son.
- El roi – 'God of Sees and Knows'[1] – God is not distant and aloof; he sees the needs of his people, hears our prayers and comes to our aid in times of trouble.

---

1   Genesis 16:13

- Yahweh-Jireh – 'The Lord Will Provide'[2] – Abraham called God by this name after God stayed his hand from sacrificing Isaac and instead provided a ram for the sacrifice. God still provides for his people's needs, ultimately giving us the Bread of Life who is Christ.
- Yahweh-Shalom – 'The Lord Our Peace'[3] – This is the name given by Gideon after the Angel of the Lord assured him he would not die as he thought he would after seeing God burn up the sacrificial offering. Yahweh is still the Lord of Peace, as David declares in Psalm 29.11 (NIV).
- Shepherd[4] and Yahweh-Rohi – the 'Shepherd of Israel'[5] – Like a shepherd who leads his sheep to good pasture and protects them from predators, the Lord is our Shepherd, supplying our needs, giving us victory over the enemy of our souls, and leading us through life.

A change in perspective

Someone once said to me that praise is not for God – it doesn't change who he is – but praise is for you as it changes how you see God. Because even when it doesn't change our circumstances, praise often changes our perspective. We read in 2 Kings 6 that God spoke to the prophet Elisha, telling him the secrets of the king of Syria (Arum). The king wasn't pleased and wanted to kill Elisha, sending a battalion out to find him. He discovered the prophet camped in a valley with his servant, and the army surrounded them. When the servant saw the army, he was understandably dismayed and asked Elisha what they should do. 'Open his eyes, LORD, so that he may see,'

2 Genesis 22.14.

3 Judges 6.24.

4 Psalm 23.1.

5 Psalm 80.1.

Elisha prayed (v. 17). When the Lord opened his eyes, the servant saw 'the hills full of horses and chariots of fire'. Elisha's servant was looking through his earthly eyes, forgetting God is at work in the spiritual realm. When we walk with thanksgiving on our lips, we enter the realm of worship. Facing a battle? Remember the words of Psalm 8.2, 'Through the praise of children and infants you have established a stronghold against your enemies, to silence the foe and the avenger.'

We too come under attack. As God's children, we have an enemy, Satan, who works against us. There are spiritual realms we don't see, but we do know that we have an enemy who wants to 'kill, steal and destroy' (John 10.10). David knew that God was his defence against his enemies – and he was someone who knew what it was like to have enemies hunting you down. He said, 'The Lord is my light and my salvation; whom shall I fear? The Lord is the strength of my life; of whom shall I be afraid?' (Psalm 27.2, KJV). When Saul was chasing after David, David ran to Samuel to hide there with the prophet (1 Samuel 19.18). Saul discovered where he was and sent men to capture him. When they arrived, rather than being able to grab David as planned, they found the presence of God was so strong that they began to prophesy too. Saul was told what happened, so he sent more men. But the same thing happened. Finally, he went himself, presumably thinking he could be the one to capture David. But 1 Samuel 19.23–24 says, 'the Spirit of God came on him, and he walked along prophesying until he came to Naioth. He stripped off his garments, and he too prophesied in Samuel's presence.' It was an unusual way for God to incapacitate one of David's enemies so he could escape, but it worked!

Let everything that has breath praise the Lord

In 1 Peter 2, we're told, 'But ye are a chosen generation, a royal priesthood, a holy nation, a peculiar people; that ye should shew forth the praises of him who hath called you out of darkness into his marvellous light.' 'Shew' means spectacle; we're called by God to create a spectacle of praise; a show the world can see that celebrates our amazing God.

David ends the book of Psalms with these words:

> Praise the Lord.
> Praise God in his sanctuary;
> praise him in his mighty heavens.
> Praise him for his acts of power;
> praise him for his surpassing greatness.
> Praise him with the sounding of the trumpet,
> praise him with the harp and lyre,
> praise him with timbrel and dancing,
> praise him with the strings and pipe,
> praise him with the clash of cymbals,
> praise him with resounding cymbals.
> Let everything that has breath praise the Lord.
> Praise the Lord.
> (Psalm 150)

Why does he command all things to praise God? Perhaps because it's not in our nature to do so – we have to be intentional to make it happen. My encouragement to you is to be intentional. In the good times and the bad. Whether you're in the belly of a whale or on dry land; chained up for the Gospel or free. Sing God's praises. Hold on to the truth of who he is and all he's done for us. Praise is a powerful weapon that can change everything.

Further resources for digging deeper

Matt Redman – *The Unquenchable Worshipper*
Warren W. Wiersbe – *Real Worship*
David F. Ford and Daniel W. Hardy – *Living in Praise*

10

Surrender

DOUG WILLIAMS

Doug is the senior pastor of Emmanuel Christian Centre, a large and thriving inner-city church in the East End of London, and leads their School of Worship ministry. He is a singer and songwriter and has played with numerous gospel artists. Doug also travels internationally to conduct leadership training sessions, church retreats and men's conferences.

Surrender is something that sounds okay in theory but is much harder in practice. Someone who knew this well was Judson W. Van DeVenter, who was born in 1855 and raised in a Christian home. After accepting Jesus as his Saviour at the age of 17, he graduated university with a degree in art and worked as an art teacher in a high school. He travelled around Europe so he could visit the various art galleries. Van DeVenter also studied and taught music, mastering 13 instruments, singing and composing music. He was heavily involved in the music ministry of his Methodist Episcopal church and found himself torn between his successful teaching career and his desire to be a part of an evangelistic team. This struggle lasted for almost five years.

In 1896, while Van DeVenter was conducting the music at a church event, he finally surrendered his desires completely to God. He decided to become a full-time evangelist, and as he submitted completely to the will of his Lord, a song was born in his heart. The words and melody of that song – 'I Surrender All' – have appeared in virtually every English hymnal and are sung in many churches to this day.[1]

---

1   <http://cmminister.blogspot.com/2016/04/story-behind-i-surrender-all-hymn.html>

Judson W. Van DeVenter taught us all a powerful lesson: it is much easier to sing about submission than it is to actually do it!

The heart of the dilemma

Why is surrender so hard? At the heart of the human dilemma called 'the fall', humankind, in wilful disobedience, chose to reject divine directive. Genesis 3 discloses the subtle nature of the serpent's corrupting counsel, the vulnerability that ensued from Eve's inaccurate recollection of God's word and the passivity of her husband, Adam, who failed to step up to the guardianship he had been tasked with. The temptation they were offered was the opportunity to be equal with God: 'you will become just like God!' (v. 5). It was, in truth, an invitation to circumvent accountability and resist submission. There can be no true worship until, and unless, this is reversed. Our struggle today is no different. The subtle temptation to circumvent true surrender to God's word and to simply do our own thing is a constant challenge.

As negative as resistance to submission is, the absence of reverence compounds the issue. In his letter to the church in Rome, Paul is very clear that human beings chose not to honour God and then directed their worship to the creation rather than the Creator (Romans 1). Compromised worship then rapidly degenerated into corrupt living. This failure to reverently honour, extol, esteem and fully recognize God for who he is, is not without destructive consequence. Therefore, all of God's redemptive activity on the earth is to evidence his desire to correct deficient human worship. In the New Testament, it is perhaps the way Jesus wonderfully modelled for us deep worship and submission to the father's will in a place called Gethsemane. Jesus often said he did nothing without reference to what would please God, even when doing so was not easy. On the night of his betrayal, he took his closet friends to Gethsemane in order to pray and prepare for his death. All the gospel writers make reference to this event (Matthew 26.36–56, Mark 14.32–52, Luke 22.40–53 and John 18.1–11), so its significance cannot be overestimated. The location, originally referred to as 'the place of pressing' (presumably due to an olive press on site) seems so appropriate for what took place that night. As Jesus contemplated the horror of sacrificially laying down his life to rescue humanity, he pleaded with God the Father that some other way to do this be found. The intensity of this struggle was seen in how urgently he asked his friends to stay awake and pray with him and his physical reaction to the weight of the moment. He felt 'pressed' and 'crushed'! We find him praying through this at least three times before he could finally say, 'Not my will but yours be done'. Is there any better example of authentic surrender? That was such a pivotal moment, but he was able to make this act of surrender when least supported, betrayed by a friend, physically exhausted and surrounded by adversaries! How did he do it? The narratives are full of clues. He fellowshipped with friends, sang hymns, prayed intensely and focussed on Scripture. The end result was his surrender – and our salvation.

Jesus would only be required to make this sacrifice once, and his surrender was key. Most contemporary believers think that any reference to 'sacrifices' for the modern church is too antiquated to have any significant application to contemporary faith expression, but I beg to differ. 'Submission in sacrifice' is still a very relevant consideration for the Church. We as Christians will never be asked to make a sacrifice in order to secure our own salvation – Jesus has done this for us once and for all – but the Christian life will involve some level of 'sacrificial' expression on our part, and this can never really be achieved without surrender.

Sacrifices for Christians today

Christian believers *are* still required to offer sacrifices to God! I know this may sound a little strange, but the Scriptures do seem to clearly indicate that this is so. We may not be required to visit a temple with an animal or grain offering, but the sacrificial references in the following texts highlight the need to consider physical disciplines, the management of money and material resource, verbal praise, service to those in need, and the pursuit of excellence in ministry as key areas of focus for every authentic worshipper to bear in mind. Just prayerfully consider the following biblical texts:

1 'Therefore, I urge you, brothers and sisters, in view of God's mercy, to offer your bodies as a living *sacrifice*, holy and pleasing to God – this is your true and proper worship' (Romans 12.1).

This verse has come up again and again in this book because it's so rich! The Apostle Paul, who wrote this passage, believed that one of the ways true spirituality could be seen was in the way that believers engage in appropriate physical disciplines. Paying attention to health concerns, resisting greed and laziness, maintaining a commitment to sexual integrity, are all disciplines to be conducted in a God-honouring, Christ-exalting manner. As such, they become expressions of true, proper – and therefore acceptable – worship.

2 'I have received full payment and have more than enough. I am amply supplied, now that I have received from Epaphroditus the gifts you sent. They are a fragrant offering, an acceptable *sacrifice*, pleasing to God. And my God will meet all your needs according to the riches of his glory in Christ Jesus' (Philippians 4.18–19, italics added).

With this second text, I am convinced that a good number of Christians are fully aware of verse 19 and its declaration that God is able to meet all of our needs. But what they fail to realize is that this promise is conveyed to a fellowship of believers who made a sacrificial investment into the support of a mission's worker and the apostolic expansion of Christian faith communities. Their management of material and financial resource in favour of kingdom objectives made them candidates for God's outstanding provision. Perhaps we can only legitimately claim verse 19 if we are willing to also engage in verse 18! How we handle money and material assets is a spiritual issue. If we fail to surrender to God here, we fail.

3 'Through Jesus, therefore, let us continually offer to God a *sacrifice* of praise – the fruit of lips that openly profess his name' (Hebrews 13.15, italics added).

Did you know that a commitment to articulated praise that tumbles unashamedly from the lips is something God views as an acceptable sacrifice? Believers are tempted to think that if such activity is outside their comfort zone or temperament profile, they get a pass from participating in this activity and can just silently hide in the crowd. But if sacrificial submission is to follow divine directive, then this passage is to be acted on. As Lou said in her chapter, you don't have to be a world-class singer to do this, but Jesus said that out of the heart's abundance the mouth speaks (Matthew 12.34). So, if worship is in your heart – in abundance – it follows that we will hear you say and sing something! I can't speak for anyone else, but my mind has wandered in some prayer meetings! But what I have discovered is that it's much harder for my words to wander than my thoughts. Being intentional at speaking out or singing out my prayers has given me a real focus – and therefore less guilt!

4 In Hebrews 13.16 we are told, 'Do not forget to do good and to share with others, for with such *sacrifices* God is pleased.' (italics added)

Acts of generous humanitarian concern are not always viewed as expressions of worship, but for the Christian believer, if the writer of the book called Hebrews is to be taken seriously, they probably should be! Proverbs 19.17 says, 'Whoever is kind to the poor lends to the Lord, and he will reward them for what they have done.' Would anybody like a reward from the Lord? Why not try lending and giving to the poor and see what happens to you! A parable Jesus told echoes this sentiment to the very first disciples, 'Then the righteous will answer him, "Lord, when did we see you hungry and feed you, or thirsty and give you something to drink? When did we see you a stranger and invite you in, or needing clothes and clothe you? When did we see you sick or in prison and go to visit you?" The King will reply, "Truly I tell you, whatever you did for one of the least of these brothers and sisters of mine, you did for me"' (Matthew 25.37–40).

God views these gestures of generosity and kindness as being done for him and to him. At times, it would appear that even those engaged in such acts are not fully aware of the implications of their own actions. Such service toward other people is recorded as giving honour to the God in whose image they have been formed. Kindness matters a lot!

5 In Romans 15.15–17, Paul references his work of outreach to Gentile communities saying, 'He gave me the priestly duty of proclaiming the gospel of God, so that the Gentiles might become *an offering acceptable to God*, sanctified by the Holy Spirit. Therefore, I glory in Christ Jesus in my service to God.' (italics added)

Paul sees *everything* he is doing as an act of sacrifice to be offered up to God in the most acceptable way. Little wonder this outstanding apostolic figure was so keen to deliver any matters in which he was engaged excellently. He wanted God to be pleased with his work and to affirm it. As a student of Scripture, he would have been well aware that there are several biblical examples of God not finding an offering acceptable such as Cain's in Genesis 4.3–5 and in Leviticus 10.1–2 when Aaron's sons made an unauthorized sacrifice. These examples make one point abundantly clear: sacrifices offered to God have to be the very best the worshipper can bring! In viewing his life's work in this manner, Paul was saying that whatever he did in Christian service had to be the very best he could offer. Contentment with low standards of discipleship and ministry were – for him, at least[2] – not an option! Such an offering would be an expression of deficient worship.

---

2   1 Corinthians 9.26–27, Galatians 6.14, Ephesians 6.19–20, Philippians 3.12–15.

There are no idle idols!

The danger is that we *do* sacrifice and surrender, just not to God. A cursory reading of the Hebraic prophets notes one large and recurring theme that they have to correct in the nation: idolatry. The ease with which ancient Israel could be seduced away from the worship of Yahweh and then align themselves with the fertility cults of the Baals (local community gods) is astounding. They were constantly given exhortations not to 'forget' God.[3] The truth is that attendance at their own temple sites and sacred festivals should have been sufficient to keep them focussed and faithful in this regard. But, alas, on far too many occasions the rampant sexual promiscuity and occultism engrained in Baal worship corrupted their conscience and compromised their worship. They replaced Yahweh with a substitute and couldn't see anything wrong in their actions. But nothing could be further from the truth. Idolatry has very costly consequences. There are key Old Testament passages that indicate this with searing clarity:

> Those who make them will be like them, and so will all who trust in them. (Psalm 115.8)

> They stirred him to jealousy with strange gods; with abominations they provoked him to anger. They sacrificed to demons that were no gods, to gods they had never known, to new gods that had come recently, whom your fathers had never dreaded. (Deuteronomy 32.16–17)

The folly of designing and venerating an idol is obvious here and may prove very insightful and helpful in our day, as we are reminded not to allow anything or anyone to occupy the place in our life that should be reserved exclusively for God. God substitutes are a

---

3   Deuteronomy 4.23, 6.10–12,8.10–14; Judges 8.33–34; 2 Kings 17.14–17,38; Psalms 50.22.

dangerous no-no! The Scriptures indicate that offering inappropriate loyalty to an idol opens the door to having your life shaped by that commitment. Furthermore, the power that seeks to shape the misguided worshipper can be very sinister indeed. Those who think that demons are merely the construct of Hollywood's horror industry may well need to remind themselves that Jesus took such matters very seriously. The need for a renewed understanding of malignant spiritual power and its dark agenda against the purpose of God cannot be underestimated. Idolatry opens a doorway to sinister and twisted spirituality.

Our idols don't have to be golden calves, totem poles, sacred rivers and trees, silver statues or magical gemstones. When we fail to allow God – and his word – first place in our lives, there are a variety of replacements that we are willing to affirm. Today, we may well need to check through the people, possessions, pleasures and positions that have become the consuming focus of our pursuits. How do they shape our thinking and decision-making? Do they draw us to God or away from him? Could we also succumb to the subtle seduction of idolatry?

It was at a Christian conference where I heard a speaker say, 'If there is something you own that you cannot give away, you don't own it, it owns you!' At first I chuckled and questioned the truth of this statement. I tried to ignore it, but it kept creeping back into my mind during the rest of the session and throughout the long drive home. There was one thing I really didn't want to give up at all: my guitar! It was my prize possession, and I loved playing it. I tried all the excuses I could think of: I used that guitar to worship God in my personal devotions; surely he didn't want me to give it away! Also, I lead worship at church, and in my small group, they would surely be disadvantaged if I didn't have it any more! Perhaps there was something else I could give instead? Something that was, of course, valuable to me (just not quite as valuable as the guitar!) I racked up so many excuses but then concluded that I was probably overthinking the whole thing, and maybe I should just put it out of my head and forget about it. But I couldn't. Those words kept reverberating in my head: *if you can't give it away, it's owning you*. Finally, I relented. 'God, you can have my guitar. There should be nothing I'm not willing to lay down if you ask me to.' Pained, I gave it to a friend, just to make sure I really could. It was a serious act of surrender and a significant challenge for somebody who loved playing as much as I did. If time would allow, I could tell you how, from that day, I have been given numerous guitars of better quality. I have since then realized that God wasn't really after my guitar but my surrender! He doesn't need another guitar, but he does want to be put first in my life.

Our idols are often the things we think we can't live without. Being willing to surrender material and financial possessions is not easy, but what proves much, much harder is to surrender people.

When I was young, I was dating a beautiful young lady who had a little boy. We seemed like a ready-made family, and I had purchased an engagement ring. But we hit a snag. The church we attended had theological convictions that were at odds with mine, and I knew that my future ministry could not be conducted in this context. We often talked about this and even spent time fasting and praying. She understood my position and agreed with its biblical premise, but she felt unable to leave the church since her family connections there were just too strong. She didn't have the courage to leave, and I didn't have the conviction to stay. My whole world went into a tailspin. I knew I had to surrender to God and terminate this relationship, but my heart was conflicted. I really tried to get God to see things differently! I knew I would miss them both but eventually had to have that tear-filled, traumatic conversation. Afterwards, I stayed in my bedroom alone for the next three days. I wept so much and discovered that surrender is costly indeed. At the end of those days, I took a trip into central London to clear my head and window shop to distract myself. There on the high street, I bumped into one of my old Bible college friends. She told me that a group of alumni was meeting for lunch and asked if I would join them. We had a great time catching up on how the years since college had been and what was taking place in our lives now. We discovered that we were all going through significant shifts and transitions, so we agreed to meet up and pray with one another. That little prayer group met faithfully for 18 months. One new face that joined that group was a lovely young lady called Joan Nelson . . . She now has my surname, and we've been married over 34 years! My act of surrender was right for both my ministry – and matrimony!

The next move is yours

If worship is a submissive and reverential response to disclosure of God, then God has to make the first move – and he has, as Scripture records the following:

'But God demonstrates his own love for us in this: *While we were still sinners,* Christ died for us' (Romans 5.8, italics added).

'And love consists in this: *not that we loved God, but that He loved us and sent His Son* as an atoning sacrifice for our sins' (1 John 4.10, italics added).

'We love, *because he first loved us'* (1 John 4.19, italics added).

Both Paul and John are in agreement that God made the first move toward humanity, in order to express his love for us. We must now respond and embrace this compassionate and redemptive overture with submission and reverence. Since submission and reverence are expressed in both attitude and action, authentic worship is expressed in the same way. First, in the attitudinal posture of the heart, and then in the sacrificial gestures at the heart of this reflection.

The principle of surrender is central to the Christian concept of worship. Truly surrendering to God's will entails the prioritizing of his will over our own. It requires us to acknowledge his sovereignty over all things – even our things! This means that we desire to honour God in every part of our personal lives, in even the smallest decisions. Christians believe that putting personal desire aside in favour of God's perfect will for our lives leads to the fullest acceptance of his calling and purpose for us. This personal surrender is expressed through our obedience to the revealed truth of Scripture and the reverence we display while doing so. This is our worship!

Further resources for digging deeper

Jack Hayford – *Manifest Presence*
Robert E. Webber – *Worship, Old & New*
Robert E. Webber – *Ancient-Future Faith*
Williams Dyrness – *Themes in Old Testament Theology*
G. K. Beale – *The Temple and the Church's Mission*
Ian Stackhouse – *The Gospel-Driven Church*
Andrew Hill – *Enter His Courts with Praise*

Part 4
THE FUTURE

The Apostle Paul writes in 2 Corinthians 4.18 that we are not to look to the things seen but to the things unseen, 'since what is seen is temporary, but what is unseen is eternal.' Worship is something we will be doing for all eternity, and it is going on right now in heavenly reality. So what can we learn if we gain a glimpse into the true reality of eternal worship? What does such worship tell us about worship right now here on earth? This is the topic of our penultimate chapter by Dr Darrell Johnson, who opens up for us the last book of the Bible – Revelation – and draws our attention to the wonder of worship seen in Chapters 4 and 5. By contrasting the picture of worship in Isaiah 6 with this scene in Revelation, Dr Johnson draws us back to the absolute centrality of Jesus and what has been accomplished on the cross. He concludes by advising us never to ask 'what did I get out of worship today?' but rather to ask 'Did I enter in? Did my heart cry, "Worthy is the Lamb who was slain?"'

We end the whole book with Tim returning for a final chapter on a future vision for worship. He calls for a 'total reformation' that must begin with our own minds and taking seriously the full surrender of Romans 12.1. Without this transformation by the Spirit in each one of us, how can the church pull away from merely imitating the ideals and opinions of contemporary culture? 'A renewed mind will lead to a renewed culture,' and only by allowing more 'freedom and space for the work of the Holy Spirit' will we accomplish this as the church of Christ. Throughout the book, we have seen how worship is the way we partner with God. This theme returns in this closing chapter – worship is not a narrow word, but a broad high-way of life with God. Tim calls us to press into our partnership with Christ, as his body, the Church, in order to create culture and image, the kingdom.

As you journey through this final section, join us in praying for a rising up of true worship around the world. Be encouraged, personally, and as a church community, that however dark things may seem, Christ shines brighter, and his light is at work in and through you as you worship him. Your worship may never be perfect, but it doesn't need to be, Jesus has won; he is our perfect sacrifice, our saviour and choirmaster. Join in with what he is doing and allow the Holy Spirit to work in and through you. The journey of worship is far more exciting and breathtaking than any of us could have imagined when we began to follow Jesus. Let us not hold back but press on in our service and adoration of God, throwing off 'everything that hinders and the sin that so easily entangles'. For worthy is the Lamb that was slain.

DR NICK DRAKE

11

Participating in a mystery

DR DARRELL JOHNSON

Darrell has been preaching the gospel for over 50 years, serving in churches in a number of Presbyterian congregations in California, Union Church of Manila in the Philippines, and the historic First Baptist Church in Vancouver, Canada. He has taught preaching for Fuller Theological Seminary, Carey Theological College in Vancouver, and Regent College in Vancouver and has authored eight books. He is currently serving as Scholar-in-Residence for The Way Church and Canadian Church Leaders Network.

Whenever we gather in the name of Jesus Christ to worship, we are participating in a mystery, even if we do not realize it at the time. The mystery? Worship of the Living God does not begin with us, and it will not end with us. May I repeat that? *Worship of the Living God does not begin with us, and it will not end with us.* When we begin a service of worship on the Lord's Day, say, at 10 a.m., worship of the Living God does not then begin with us at 10 a.m., and it will not end with us at 11:30 a.m. To enter into a time of worship in this earthly dimension of our existence is to enter a service *already in progress* in the heavenly realms, because there is always a worship service taking place in heaven.

As the hymn so beautifully puts it:

> Joyful, joyful we adore Thee,
>> God of glory, Lord of love . . .

Stars and angels sing around Thee . . .
Centre of unbroken praise.[1]

Of that worship already in progress, the Scriptures give us a number of snapshots so that we, in the earthly dimension, can know how to worship in ways that please the Living God. Not that we are to copy what we see and hear; that would not be possible. But what we see and hear in heavenly worship helps shape and empower earthly worship. 'On earth as it is in heaven,' as Jesus teaches us to pray.

The two clearest pictures of heavenly worship are given to us by the Prophet Isaiah in Chapter 6 of his massive work (happening in 740 BC) and the Apostle John in the fourth and fifth chapters of Revelation,[2] happening in 92 AD.[3]

Take a few moments to read each of these pictures of heavenly worship.

In the year of King Uzziah's death I saw the Lord sitting on a throne, lofty and exalted, with the train of His robe filling the temple. Seraphim stood above Him, each having six wings: with two he covered his face, and with two he covered his feet, and with two he flew. And one called out to another and said,
'Holy, Holy, Holy, is the LORD of hosts,
The whole earth is full of His glory.'
And the foundations of the thresholds trembled at the voice of him who called out, while the temple was filling with smoke. Then I said,
'Woe is me, for I am ruined!
Because I am a man of unclean lips,
And I live among a people of unclean lips;

---

1 'Joyful, joyful, we adore thee' written by Henry J. van Dyke, 1907.

2 Also see Revelation 7.9–17; 11.15–18; 15.2–4; 19.1–7.

3 Although some scholars suggest 67 AD, the actual date does not affect the point that I'm making about worship.

For my eyes have seen the King, the LORD of hosts.'
Then one of the seraphim flew to me with a burning coal in his
hand, which he had taken from the altar with tongs. He touched
my mouth *with it* and said, 'Behold, this has touched your lips;
and your iniquity is taken away and your sin is forgiven.'
(Isaiah 6.1–6, NASB)

After these things I looked, and behold, a door *standing* open in
heaven, and the first voice which I had heard, like *the sound* of a
trumpet speaking with me, said, "Come up here, and I will show you
what must take place after these things." Immediately I was in the
Spirit; and behold, a throne was standing in heaven, and One sitting
on the throne. And He who was sitting *was* like a jasper stone and
a sardius in appearance; and *there was* a rainbow around the throne,
like an emerald in appearance. Around the throne *were* twenty-four
thrones; and upon the thrones *I saw* twenty-four elders sitting,
clothed in white garments, and golden crowns on their heads.

The Throne and Worship of the Creator

Out from the throne came flashes of lightning and sounds and
peals of thunder. And *there were* seven lamps of fire burning
before the throne, which are the seven Spirits of God; and
before the throne *there was something* like a sea of glass,
like crystal; and in the center and around the throne, four
living creatures full of eyes in front and behind. The first
creature *was* like a lion, and the second creature like a calf, and
the third creature had a face like that of a man, and the fourth
creature *was* like a flying eagle. And the four living creatures,
each one of them having six wings, are full of eyes around and
within; and day and night they do not cease to say,
"HOLY, HOLY, HOLY *is* THE LORD GOD, THE ALMIGHTY, WHO
WAS AND WHO IS AND WHO IS TO COME."

And when the living creatures give glory and honor and thanks to Him who sits on the throne, to Him who lives forever and ever, the twenty-four elders will fall down before Him who sits on the throne, and will worship Him who lives forever and ever, and will cast their crowns before the throne, saying,

"Worthy are You, our Lord and our God, to receive glory and honor and power; for You created all things, and because of Your will they existed, and were created."

The Book with Seven Seals

I saw in the right hand of Him who sat on the throne a book written inside and on the back, sealed up with seven seals. And I saw a strong angel proclaiming with a loud voice, "Who is worthy to open the book and to break its seals?" And no one in heaven or on the earth or under the earth was able to open the book or to look into it. Then I *began* to weep greatly because no one was found worthy to open the book or to look into it; and one of the elders said to me, "Stop weeping; behold, the Lion that is from the tribe of Judah, the Root of David, has overcome so as to open the book and its seven seals."

And I saw between the throne (with the four living creatures) and the elders a Lamb standing, as if slain, having seven horns and seven eyes, which are the seven Spirits of God, sent out into all the earth. And He came and took the book out of the right hand of Him who sat on the throne. When He had taken the book, the four living creatures and the twenty-four elders fell down before the Lamb, each one holding a harp and golden bowls full of incense, which are the prayers of the saints. And they sang a new song, saying,

"Worthy are You to take the book and to break its seals; for You were slain, and purchased for God with Your blood *men* from every tribe and tongue and people and nation.

"You have made them *to be* a kingdom and priests to our God; and they will reign upon the earth."

Angels Exalt the Lamb

Then I looked, and I heard the voice of many angels around the throne and the living creatures and the elders; and the number of them was myriads of myriads, and thousands of thousands, saying with a loud voice,
"Worthy is the Lamb that was slain to receive power and riches and wisdom and might and honor and glory and blessing."
And every created thing which is in heaven and on the earth and under the earth and on the sea, and all things in them, I heard saying,
"To Him who sits on the throne, and to the Lamb, *be* blessing and honor and glory and dominion forever and ever."
And the four living creatures kept saying, "Amen." And the elders fell down and worshiped.
(Revelation 4–5, NASB)

As you read the two heavenly worship scenes, you no doubt noticed how similar they are and, quite possibly, you recognize how they have shaped the Church's worship for centuries. Yet, although similar, there are of course some major differences. Because, from the time of the Isaiah 6 picture to the time of the Revelation 4–5 picture, something changed. Between 740 BC and 92 AD, something happened on earth that changed heavenly worship, and when we begin to grasp this change in heavenly worship, our earthly worship changes!

To explore this more, let's look at two key questions. Question one: what is the same? Question two: what is different? The difference is what makes Christian worship Christian.

What is the same?

1 God is on the throne

In 740 BC, Isaiah says, 'In the year that King Uzziah died, I saw the LORD[4] sitting on a throne.' Whereas, in 92 AD, John says, 'I was in the Spirit on the Lord's day; and look![5] A throne was standing in heaven.' It's the same throne 830 years later. Defying all assaults against it, surviving all coup attempts, and still standing, while thousands of other thrones have collapsed before it. Isaiah also says, 'I saw the LORD sitting on the throne.' Whereas John says, 'Behold! Look! A throne with Someone sitting on it.' The throne is occupied! There is a headquarters of the universe, and it is not vacant. It is not up for grabs. Someone is sitting on the throne!

It's important to note that no other prophet dates events from the death of a king; they always say, 'in the xth year of such-and-such a king.' The year 740 BC was a terrifying one. Judah was the next nation-state in the line of Assyria's marching advance. And then Uzziah died. The year 740 BC was full of fear. Ever had such a year? I am writing this in 2020, a very unsettling year for the whole world, chiefly, but not only, because of the Covid-19 pandemic. When John wrote in 92 AD, it was a time when persecution once again intensified as the Roman Emperor Domitian heated up his reign of terror. The beloved Apostle John was arrested and shipped off to the prison island of Patmos, to, in the words of Thomas Torrance, 'rot and bleach on the

---

4 The title LORD, all in capital letters, is a reverent rendering of the name Yahweh, the name by which the Living God chooses to be known and called, the name he revealed to Moses in the burning bush (Exodus 3.13–15). In the rest of this chapter, I will periodically use the name.

5 Look! Often simply rendered 'Behold' or 'Lo'. It is not just a nice rhetorical devise to enliven the text. It is a command. It turns out to be one of the two great commands of the last book of the Bible, the other being, 'Do not be afraid.' And it turns out we live out, 'Do not be afraid,' by living out, 'Look!' Trace the use of the command 'Look' through the New Testament, and you will see it regularly introduces a surprise, pointing to something we would not expect and would have never deduced on our own.

rocks.'[6] The Emperor Domitian asserted his rage, but couldn't overcome the Emperor of Glory.

In the time between Isaiah's words and John's, China had gone through at least 11 major dynasty changes; 11 major enthronings and dethronings. Since 740 BC, we have witnessed the coming and going of empire after empire, kingdom after kingdom, government after government, administration after administration. From Rome and all her Caesars, to Adolph Hitler and the Italian Empire of Benito Mussolini – names that used to make us shudder – gone.

When all other thrones disintegrate, there is one throne that remains, and we have every reason to believe it will continue to stand! (It would be wholly appropriate to say out loud, 'Amen!' if you would like!)

2 Holy, holy, holy

In Isaiah 6 and Revelation 4–5, God is worshipped as being 'Holy, holy, holy'. Not just 'holy'; it's always three times because the One who sits on the throne is three in one. The LORD on the throne is the Triune God. The essential character of the Triune God is holy, implying awesome beauty and consuming purity, both undiminished by time. Just as beautiful in 92 AD as he was in 740 BC. Just as pure in 92 AD as he was in 740 BC. The word holy also implies 'other than'. Although we are made in his image (Genesis 1.26–27), he is not made in our image (Exodus 20.4). 'Wholly other' than us, he is 'Holy, holy, holy'.

3 The living creatures

In Isaiah, we read, 'And there were seraphim, each having six wings.' And in Revelation, it says, 'And around the throne are living creatures, each having six wings.' In both pictures, creatures

---

6 Thomas Torrance, *The Apocalypse Today*, (London, J. Clark, 1959)

are attending to the throne. 'Day and night they do not cease,' says John. Never tiring of the repetition. Over and over and over and over. 'Holy, holy, holy.' 'Qadosh, qadosh, qadosh.' 'Sanctus, sanctus, sanctus.' Day and night. 'Holy, holy, holy.' Day after day, night after night, week after week, month after month, decade after decade, century after century. 'Holy, holy, holy.'

Something changed

Both times, we see a throne with someone sitting on it, attended to by creatures who cannot stop repeating the song, but in the Revelation picture, a number of things are different. Between 740 BC and 92 AD, something changed. Oh, how it changed!

There are three differences to note between the passages.

1 After John sees the throne, he sees, to his surprise, 24 other, smaller thrones. What gives? Are rival thrones trying to move in and take over? No! The Living God has chosen to set up other thrones around him. The Living God has chosen to bring others in on his governing of the world.[7]

Why 24? It's 2 x 12, with 12 representing God's people before Jesus's incarnation, death and resurrection and another 12 representing God's people after Jesus's incarnation, death and resurrection. The fulfilment of Jesus's promise, 'You will reign with me.' Indeed, the fulfilment of God's original creation intention for us: to exercise dominion with him over the created order (Genesis 1.28–30).

God's throne cannot be toppled and neither can the small thrones. Through all the ups and downs of history, the church of Jesus Christ

---

7 Thus the promise Jesus makes to his church in Revelation 2.26–27; 3.21. See also Luke 19.12–27.

remains. It is his promise: 'I will build my church, and the gates of hell will not prevail against it' (Matthew 16.18). Oh, the gates of hell have tried, and go on trying, but they have not won. And they will not win.

2 Let's look at those attending to the throne; they are different. Specifically, they act differently.

'Seraphim with six wings. And with two they cover their faces' (Isaiah 6.2). Why cover? Because of the awesome beauty of the One on the throne. Because of the awesome purity of the One on the throne. As mere creatures, they could not handle the beauty and purity. Which is why Isaiah himself cries out, 'Woe is me, for my eyes have seen the King, and I am ruined' (v. 5). A mere creature, and a sinful mere creature at that, not able to handle the presence of Holiness.

John said, 'Each having six wings' but makes no mention of covering eyes. Instead, John says the creatures with six wings 'are full of eyes around and within.' In 740 BC, they could not handle the sight, so they covered their eyes; in 92 AD, they not only don't cover their eyes, they are full of eyes! Goodness gracious!

Something must have happened to allow the creatures to behold holiness. Something must have happened to allow the creatures to stand in the presence of holiness without being undone! What was it? We come to the heart of the change in heavenly worship, and every time I see it, my heart bursts for joy!

'Stop weeping; behold (look!), the Lion has overcome . . . And I saw in the middle of the throne a Lamb' (Revelation 5.5; 6).

There are two words in the Greek New Testament that are translated 'lamb'. One is *amnos,* referring to an adult sheep. It is the word John the Baptist used when he saw Jesus of Nazareth coming down the road and exclaimed, 'Behold, the Lamb of God who takes away the sin of the world' (John 1.29). The other Greek word is *arnion,* referring to a little lamb, which is what is used here. This is the Virgin Mary's little lamb. Notice it says the lamb was in the middle, which can only mean in the middle of the One who sits on the throne. Right? How can the lamb be in the middle of the throne unless he is in the middle of the Almighty One? Oh, my!

And this lamb was 'as if slain'. THAT is what happened! The Lamb was slain. Jesus of Nazareth was slain. The Lamb of God who takes away the sin of the world was slain. And that changes everything!

It is why the 24 other thrones are there. They represent the Lamb's people. The people he bought with the price of his blood.

And it is why those attending to the throne need no longer cover their eyes! Something has been done for creation that enables mere creatures to be in the presence of blazing beauty and burning purity and not get fried! Jesus Christ has taken away our sin!

And that change completely changes the dynamics of heavenly worship. The whole feel, tone, tenor of worship changes. In 740 BC, the creatures hide their faces. In 92 AD, the creatures open their eyes and point humanity to the Lamb who stands in the middle of everything. This accounts for the next, crucial difference.

3 Human language in the two pictures is different.

Isaiah, having been ushered into the presence of God, cries, 'woe!' 'Woe is me!' John, having been ushered into the presence of God, cries, 'worthy!' 'Worthy is the Lamb who was slain.' Before the death and resurrection of Mary's little lamb, the posture and language of worship is fear. 'Woe! I am such a miserable sinner. I have fallen short of the glory of God.' After the death and resurrection of Mary's little lamb, the posture and language of worship is joy. 'Worthy! You are worthy! You have made it possible for me to be here!'

It's true that when we enter into the unveiled presence of the beauty and purity of the Holy God, our immediate instinct is still, 'woe'. Peter, the fisherman, encounters Jesus on the shore of the Sea of Galilee, and his first instinct is, 'depart from me for I am a sinful man O Lord' (Luke 5. 8). But when we see in the middle of all that awesome beauty and purity the crucified Jesus, before 'woe' can come out of our mouths, 'worthy' takes over. For we are no longer the issue; we never have been. He is the issue. 'Worthy!' 'My debt You paid, my death You died, that I might live!'[8]

Everything changed

Everything changed because something wonderful happened. In Isaiah 6, we see that at the centre of the universe is holiness, unspeakable beauty and purity. In Revelation 4–5, at the centre of all that holiness is unspeakable mercy and grace, for in the middle – in the middle! – of all that holiness is the Lamb who died to take away my sin and your sin. It is safe to press into the heart of the Holy God. For at the heart of the Holy God is the Lamb who calls us to come in! I belong, you belong! (It is wholly appropriate for you to shout out loud 'Thank you, thank you!' if you would like!)

'Worthy!'

Revelation 5.12 says, 'Worthy is the Lamb that was slain to receive power and riches and wisdom and might and honour and glory and blessing.' Why put it that way? Why heap up all those words? And why those particular words? Because John is making a statement to his contemporaries. He is making a statement about the Roman throne which, in its arrogance, thought itself to be the throne of the universe. (So contemporary, no?) By 92 AD, Roman emperors were thinking and speaking of themselves as divine. Domitian wanted to be called 'Dominus et Deus' ('Lord and God'). Thus, when the Emperor entered the Senate chambers, all in attendance were to rise and sing, 'Worthy are you to receive power

---

8   Graham Kendrick, "Amazing Love (My Lord, What Love Is This)", Make Way Music, 1989.

and riches and wisdom and might and honour and glory and blessing.' 'No,' says John. And all of creation joins him: 'No'. No Caesar,
no Emperor, Roman or British or German or Chinese or American – no human leader is worthy to receive power and riches and
wisdom and might and honour and glory and blessing. There is only
one who is worthy of such unbridled adoration and unqualified ac-
claim: the one who stands in the middle of the one who sits on the
throne that cannot be moved.

So, worship on the Lord's Day does not begin with us, and it will
not end with us. Which means the question to ask after any of our
services of worship is not, 'What did I get out of it?' I am not the
point. You are not the point. None of us is the point. The question to
ask after any of our services of worship is, 'Did I enter in? Did I enter
into the mystery? Did I enter into the worship that never ceases? Did
I enter into the change that has taken place in heavenly worship? Did
I realize that the Lamb is at the centre of it all?'

The question to ask is, 'Did my heart cry, "Worthy is the Lamb
Who was slain!"?' One day it will be the cry of the whole universe!

Resources for digging deeper

Glenn Packiam – *Worship and the World to Come: Exploring Christian Hope in Contemporary Worship*

12
A vision for worship

TIM HUGHES

Standing in a run-down gymnasium, I was leading a large group of men in worship. I've led worship at hundreds of events all over the world, but this was unlike any I'd ever been involved in. Here in front of me were five hundred men, all dressed in white, serving time in a maximum security prison in the heart of Texas, USA.

Passing through various security check points as we entered the prison, the mood among the band had become increasingly sombre. We were all apprehensive and unsure as to what we should expect. How would we be treated? How would these men respond to our leading them in worship? As the gym filled up and people took their seats, my mind began to wander. The men before me had caused utter devastation and pain to thousands of people. Murderers, rapists, paedophiles, armed robbers, deceivers – a horrific catalogue of crime and depravity. I was struggling to see how this room, full of people that had experienced and engaged in such evil, could become a holy sanctuary of worship. But what happened next marked me forever. As we began, the room erupted in joyful singing. There was such passion, love and hope; a tangible sense of God's Spirit with us. As we sang the hymn 'Amazing Grace', with hands held high, many faces were wet with tears as the immortal lines were sung:

> Amazing Grace how sweet the sound.
> To save a wretch like me.

> I once was lost but now I'm found,
> Was blind but now I see.

Many of these men had encountered God's love and mercy while serving time in prison and had been irrevocably changed. Whereas, in the physical, they were locked up and incarcerated – and many were serving life sentences – these men were free. They were forgiven and liberated by the atoning blood of Jesus. And because of this glorious truth, they were overflowing with hope and joy. It was in this prison in Texas that I understood afresh the power of worship. The reality that an encounter with God and a living relationship with him can transform the darkest of places.

In knowing and being known by the God of all creation, we experience a love like no other, a love that changes us from the inside out. It's in worship that we step into a new reality that shifts our perspective to understand that there is no human being beyond redemption and no situation too bleak for Christ to shine.

The glory of Christ

At the start of 2020, the world was hit by the grim reality of Covid-19. It had an extraordinary impact, wreaking havoc with our health, hospitals, economy, places of work, mental health and everyday freedoms. During those first few weeks when we in the UK were put into lockdown, in the midst of finding new ways of working by Zoom and juggling the home schooling of kids, I started studying the book of Revelation[1]. Here we see the Apostle John, by now physically frail, in his mid-80s, exiled on the Island of Patmos. Legend had it that he had been boiled in oil before being left alone on this island to die. Perhaps, though, John's greatest suffering was the knowledge that the Church

---

1   As part of this study I thoroughly recommend Darrell Johnson's excellent commentary, 'Discipleship On The Edge', Regent College Publishing, 2004.

and the people he so dearly loved were being tortured and persecuted on account of their faith. Many were being martyred, fed to lions and burnt alive. As many as forty thousand Christians were thought to have been killed by Domitian, the Emperor of Rome. So here's John, in his own form of torment and lockdown, physically in pain, emotionally grief-stricken, feeling helpless. And what does he do? He worships.

'On the Lord's Day I was in the Spirit' (Revelation 1.10). On the day where the early Church would gather in prayer and worship, John joins with them, albeit alone. And it's here, in the most unlikely of places, where God reveals himself in a way that would transform John, but would, more profoundly, transform the world.

Throughout his years, John would have experienced the love and mercy of Jesus. Watching him up close heal the sick, embrace the outsider and ultimately lay down his life on a cross. He witnessed the resurrection and ascension of Jesus, but here in Patmos, John's eyes are opened to see Christ in all his glory. The view before him was so overwhelming that human language became woefully insufficient. Hair white '*like*' wool . . . eyes '*like*' a blazing fire . . . feet '*like*' bronze glowing in a furnace . . . his voice '*like*' the sound of rushing waters . . . his face '*like*' the sun shining in all its brilliance (Revelation 1.14–16). Overwhelmed and undone, John falls at Jesus's feet as though dead. Years earlier, John had been so comfortable in Jesus's presence that he reclined closely next to him[2]. But here the sight of Christ in all his majesty was just too much for John to deal with. He hits the deck, and now the Creator of the heavens and the earth, perfect and holy, the one who was and is and is to come, reaches out and intimately places his hand on John and utters the stunning words, 'Do not be afraid. I am the First and the Last. I am the Living One; I was dead, and behold I am alive for ever and ever!' (Revelation 1.17–18).

---

2   John 13:23 "One of them, the disciple whom Jesus loved [John], was reclining next to him."

In the bleakest of moments, John encounters Jesus in all his brilliance, splendour and glory and realizes Christ has overcome. The power of death and the problem of sin, dealt with. Life in all its fullness and abundance can now be ours for eternity. And this truth wasn't just a private moment for John; the book of Revelation has inspired the church for over two thousand years with hope and confidence for what is to come. The Lamb is victorious! All things will be made new and restored. Everything will be put right, and one day soon we will stand before the Lord and for for ever and a day, all suffering, pain and grief will cease.

In worship, heaven's reality becomes our reality. You see, worship is not about escaping the real world. No, in worship, we introduce the real world. We all face mountains – mountains of despair, sickness, disappointment, relational breakdown, financial strain and loss. In worship, we don't deny the existence of these mountains, rather we acknowledge a greater existence. A God who rules and reigns, who stands with us at all times, one who will never leave our side. We might face great loss during the years we live here on earth, but ultimately nothing can separate us from the love of God.

Shape or be shaped?

Throughout this book, Romans 12.1 has been frequently referenced:

'Therefore, I urge you, brothers and sisters, in view of God's mercy, to offer your bodies as a living sacrifice, holy and pleasing to God – this is your true and proper worship.'

As we draw to a close, I want us to look at the verse that immediately follows:

'Do not conform to the pattern of this world, but be transformed by the renewing of your mind. Then you will be able to test and approve what God's will is – his good, pleasing and perfect will' (Romans 12.2).

Daily, we are being shaped. Culture is squeezing us into its mould. The values of the age around image, success, sexuality and money are bombarding and discipling us. The danger in the Church is that we underestimate the power and influence culture has over us, unaware of how we are being shaped. The author Eugene Peterson uses the picture of a fish in water, suggesting that it is as hard for us to recognize the world's temptations going on all around us, as it is for fish to recognize the impurities in the water all around them[3].

Billions of dollars are being spent by tech companies to find ways to engage us in various products and ways of thinking. Endless algorithms are at work to predict our behaviour and desires. More than that, they are seeking to shape our desires and habits. On our own, it's not a fair fight.

Paul, in writing this letter to the church in Rome, is highly aware of the power of culture. At the time, the laws, values and practises of Rome were being forcefully exported and implemented all over the world under the rule and reign of Caesar. And so to the early Church, who were asking the question 'What does it look like to follow Jesus and his teachings in Rome?' Paul says, 'Do not *conform* to the pattern of the world . . . rather be *transformed*!'

I love how the Passion Translation puts it: 'Stop imitating the ideals and opinions of the culture around you, but be inwardly transformed by the Holy Spirit through a total reformation of how you think.'

We need a total reformation. A complete transforming of our minds and hearts. Only then can we see the world change. It's a transformed mind that will lead to a transformed world. A renewed mind that will lead to a renewed culture. It's in being shaped by Jesus that we begin to shape culture. And this all takes place in worship. As Richard Foster writes in his brilliant book *The Celebration of Discipline*, 'To stand before the Holy One of eternity is to change. Resentments cannot be held with the same tenacity when we enter his gracious light . . . In worship an increased power steals its way

---

3   Eugene Peterson, *Long Obedience In The Same Direction*, InterVaristy Press, 2000, P.2.

into the heart sanctuary, an increased compassion grows in the soul. To worship is to change.'[4]

Dietrich Bonhoeffer lived during the rise of Hitler and the Third Reich. In seeing how the church in Germany was compromising and cooperating with the Reich, he gathered around him young men and women to disciple them. He realized, bottom line, this was a worship issue. The call was to draw Christians to radical love and obedience to Christ. A small movement was formed with Bonhoeffer's students being committed to worship, the reading of Scripture, prayer and sacred rhythms and practices. Many of these disciples were tested, some being arrested and even murdered by the Gestapo. Due to the passion and devotion of Bonhoeffer's students, many accused them of fanaticism. When challenged by one friend, Bonhoeffer took him for a walk up to the brow of a hill. Before them, they could see a vast plain with squadrons of German soldiers training for war. Pleading with his friend, he made the point that before them was a new generation of Germans who were being trained for a kingdom of hardness and cruelty. A generation who would go to great lengths to bring about Hitler's vision for a new world. The only hope Bonhoeffer could see were disciples who were completely sold out for Christ. On reflecting on this story, Jon Tyson remarks in his book *Beautiful Resistance*, 'this must be stronger than that.[5]' The love of Christ and commitment to his ways must be stronger than the pull of the world to its values and ideals. Jesus's disciples must be willing to confront the evil of the age and be prepared to stand for truth and love. To quote A.W. Tozer, 'to be so hopelessly in love with God that the idea of a transfer of affection never even remotely exists.'[6]

When it comes to culture, the Church has often struggled in its response. Often we've simply *condemned* culture, withdrawing

---

4   Richard Foster, *The Celebration of Discipline*, Hodder & Stoughton, 1989, P.214.

5   Jon Tyson, *Beautiful Resistance*, Multnomah, 2020, P. 2.

6   A. W. Tozer, *Whatever Happened To Worship?*, Christian Publications, Inc., 1985, p. 33.

from the world, wagging our fingers from afar in judgement. At worst, the world is seen as a bad and dangerous place, and Christians need to retreat to remain safe and pure. But when we respond in this way, the Church becomes periphery to the world, irrelevant and detached.

In Jesus, though, we see a very different way, 'For God did not send his Son into the world to condemn the world, but to save the world through him' (John 3.17). Jesus took on human flesh and immersed himself into the very heart of the world, not to condemn it, but rather to save it. The incarnate Jesus came to show that there is a different way to live! With Christ alive in us, we don't need to withdraw and condemn the world.

On the other hand, we've also historically seen the Church respond by copying culture and the ways of the world. We're more influenced by the leadership models of Apple or Amazon than we are by the ways of Jesus. In a drive to make the Church relevant and accessible, we jettison the hard teaching of Jesus around money, sexuality and justice. We choose not to speak on sin and holiness for fear of offending. The result is that the lives of Christians bear no distinction from anyone else's.

The Church isn't called to run away from the world, or to fold into the ways of the world; rather, we are called to partner with Christ in creating culture. We are called and set apart to usher in the kingdom of God. A world of love, beauty, forgiveness, kindness, joy, humility, sacrifice and peace. As my friend Alan Scott writes,

> The church of the future will neither practice cultural avoidance nor hunger for cultural relevance. It will no longer be intimidated or impressed by culture. Churches in the future will know that we can't bring life to the city by avoiding the city or by becoming the city. The church of the future will move beyond seeking cultural relevance toward releasing culture.[7]

---

7   Alan Scott, from article, 'The Church of the Future Part 1,' <https://www.alan-scott.org>.

The early Church didn't import the culture of the world into the Church; they exported the culture of God's kingdom into the world. God's vision for our lives is that we would be so transformed by his love that we would live in such a way that people around us are transformed.

Let me say it again, this happens in worship.

It's during time in God's presence that our minds are renewed to bring about the renewal of all things. Each day, as we reflect on God's word, as we choose to fill our hearts with thanksgiving for all Christ has won for us, as we invite the Spirit to fill us afresh, our minds are being renewed. The force of culture loses its grip on us, and we become shaped by Christ to shape culture.

As Paul says to the church in Rome, we are to be *transformed* by the renewing of our mind. The Greek word used for 'transformed' here in Romans 12 appears only three other times in the New Testament. Twice it is used in describing the transfiguration of Jesus, but the final time it is used in 2 Corinthians 3.18, 'And all of us, with unveiled faces, seeing the glory of the Lord as though reflected in a mirror, are being transformed into the same image from one degree of glory to another; for this comes from the Lord, the Spirit.'

As we behold Jesus, we begin to reflect him. We begin to be transformed into his likeness, allowing the power of his Holy Spirit to change and transform us. That's why, as the great Swiss Reformed theologian Karl Barth said, 'Christian worship is the most momentous, most urgent, most glorious action that can take place in human life.'[8] As we worship, we become more like Jesus, and it's in worship that we are empowered to do all the glorious things Jesus did.

---

8   Cited in J.J von Allmen, *Worship: It's Theology and Practice*, trans Harold Knight & W Fletcher Fleet (New York: Oxford), 1965, p.13.

Rewilding

As we come to the end of this book, I'd love to share a few personal reflections on what I see and sense God calling his Church into, regarding worship. I've had the great joy of leading worship for nearly 25 years, during which time I've served in three local churches[9]. I've been blessed beyond measure to travel extensively and lead at huge conferences and globally known churches within multiple different contexts and denominations. As I reflect on years gone by and expectantly look to what is to come, I believe we need to see more freedom and space for the work of the Holy Spirit in our worship.

Knepp is a 3,500-acre estate in West Sussex, in the UK. In 2001, after years of the land being intensively farmed, a decision was made to let the land run wild in a pioneering project known as rewilding. The driving principle was to establish a thriving ecosystem where nature was given as much freedom as possible. A natural process was encouraged rather than the historic obsessing over goals and outcomes. Using grazing animals as the drivers to create new habitats, alongside the restoration of dynamic natural water courses, the project has seen remarkable increases in wildlife. Extremely rare species such as nightingales, peregrine falcons and purple emperor butterflies can now be found, while the population of more common species has exploded. The land is now brimming with life, and consequently many other areas have engaged in the rewilding of their land[10].

I believe there is a rewilding process that needs to take place in our churches. At times, our worship services have become so carefully organized and curated, much like the intensively farmed land of the Knepp Estate, that we've lost any sense of being surprised by God's Spirit. We've held control tightly, with every minute of a

---

9 I've had the wonderful privilege of serving as a Worship Pastor at both Soul Survivor Watford with Mike Pilavachi and at Holy Trinity Brompton with Nicky Gumbel. I now have the great joy of leading with my wife Gas Street Church in Birmingham.

10 To find out more about this rewilding process visit Knepp.co.uk.

Sunday service being accounted for. Of course, we need order and structure in our worship, as the Apostle Paul teaches in 1 Corinthians 14, and, yes, I passionately believe the Spirit breathes on and works through our prayerful preparation. But I am convinced the great need for the Church today is to see the Spirit of the Living God being given freedom to lead and move. We need more disruption. More honest and passionate expressions of our love and devotion. More mess. More risk.

When we look at the Acts of the Apostles, we see remarkable things happened as the early Church gathered in worship. The room would shake as the Spirit was poured out, the sick were healed and people were emboldened to carry the gospel all over the world. I've seen glimpses of this today, but surely there has to be more! Don't you long for the highlight of a Sunday gathering not to simply be a great new song, or a brilliant preach, but rather the demonstration of God's power and love through people finding faith, being healed and set free?

One night in January 2009, an eight-year-old girl named Anna went running into her parent's room. Her face was distorted, her speech slurred and she began to shake uncontrollably as a fit seized her body. Her terrified parents rushed her to the nearest hospital where, after days of intrusive tests, they received the horrendous news that their precious daughter had severe epilepsy. With large doses of medication, she was able to return to school, but life was far from normal; frequent fits and seizures would see Anna rushed to hospital. Constant fear stalked the family as they tried to adjust with the pain of this new reality.

It was November 2010 when Anna and her mother attended a Worship Central event in Bristol. During the worship, we felt the Spirit lead us to pray for healing, and so we invited people forward for prayer. Without hesitation, Anna bolted to the front. One of our team asked how they could pray for her, to which Anna replied, 'I've got epilepsy and I don't want it any more!' The team prayed for her, and at the end she said thank you and left. That was it. Or so we thought.

A few years later, Anna's mother emailed me to say, 'I'm not sure quite what happened that night, but all I know is she hasn't had a seizure since . . . Of course, no big signpost arrives in the sky announcing "don't panic: that was the last one" – it's a slow, day-by-day hoping and praying and watching and fearing and hoping again. Every single day is a little miracle that gets ticked off. One year, two years got ticked off. Last Christmas, Anna began being weaned off her medication; this September, she was officially signed off by the paediatric consultant. And this week, we celebrate three full clear years.'

I have no idea what songs we sang that night or who preached, but I'll never forget this stunning story of God's kindness and power to heal his precious daughter. What would happen if we would let go of the reins? Prepare diligently but hold our plans lightly, allowing space for the Spirit's leading. What devotion and love would rise up if we would not just rely on a scripted response in worship, but allowed the raw mess of who we are to encounter the glorious nature of who God is?

The other area of rewilding I believe we need to see is around diversity. We live in divided and fractured times. Politically, nationally, economically – we are split over race, gender and the environment, alongside many other issues. The horror of racism is still so devastatingly present, as seen in the callous murder of George Floyd. The last six months have led many, including me, to reflect and repent on where we've missed so much. Where we've failed to see patterns of thinking in us that have exacerbated divides, where we've failed to stand up for our brothers and sisters in Christ and where we've been slow to celebrate diversity in our churches and communities.

Scripture is incredibly clear: God loves diversity. God's creation is packed full of colour, beauty and variety. We are all created equally in his image, and every one of us carries the likeness of God. Scripture is also very clear on God's great love of unity. His great longing is that we would dwell together in harmony, living as one. We see a glimpse of all that is to come in Revelation, as we catch an insight into the worship of heaven: 'After this I looked, and there before me was a great multitude that no one could count, from every nation, tribe, people and language, standing before the throne and before the Lamb' (Revelation 7.9).

In heaven, we see diversity not simply being tolerated but being celebrated. For eternity, we will all gather – a great multitude made up of every nation, tribe and tongue – before Jesus, united in wonder, love and praise.

There are many secular organizations trying to challenge great injustices, attempting to pull people together. There is a lot of talk of shifting power, claiming rights and redressing wrongs. While there is much important work to be done, it is the worship of Jesus Christ that ultimately unites us. And, for this reason, it is the Church that should truly demonstrate to a fractured world what it looks like to be diverse but unified. Imagine how our churches could model something so different from the way of the world. Oh that our church gatherings would be places where all people are welcomed and loved, where our worshipping expression was free and diverse!

On 14 April 1906, a group of people, led by William Seymour, met in an old run-down Methodist church on Azusa Street in California, America. William Seymour was born to recently freed slaves and grew up in a time of great racial injustice and violence. The Ku Klux Klan were running riot, and the Jim Crow laws enforced racial segregation. But here on Azusa Street, as the Spirit of God was remarkably poured out, men, women and children of every race, colour and creed, the rich and the poor, all came to worship and experience the power of God. The meetings were revolutionary in that they defied racial segregation laws; everyone gathered together as one. The services would often last for 10–12 hours, sometimes for several days and nights as the Spirit ran wild, bringing healing and salvation to thousands. But the most significant result of this revival was the many men and woman who were sent out as missionaries all throughout the world. It also became a catalytic moment for Pentecostalism to explode worldwide. Today it is estimated that there are nearly 300 million Pentecostal Christians globally. Many would trace their roots back to the revival that took place in 1906 in a dilapidated building on Azusa Street.

How I long to see our churches join together as one, modelling repentance and forgiveness, pursuing the necessary learning of how to truly love and accept one another. I believe as we join together, unified through Jesus, then God will pour out his blessing upon us. William Seymour is credited as saying, 'I can say, through the power of the Spirit, that where God can get a people that will come together in one accord and one mind in the Word of God, the baptism of the Holy Ghost will fall upon them.'[11]

We are living in a time of both extraordinary challenge and extraordinary opportunity. No doubt the world is getting darker, and yet it's in worship that the light of Christ shines brighter, dispelling the darkness. William Temple, a former Archbishop of Canterbury, during a radio broadcast to the nation at the outbreak of the Second World War, stated, 'This world can be saved from political chaos and collapse by one thing only, and that is worship.'[12] No song or liturgy can bring such salvation, only the love and power of Christ. It's in worship that our minds are renewed, our hearts set ablaze and our perspective for ever shifted. It's in worship we step in to our great call to be bearers of light and beacons of hope.

Resources for digging deeper

Ruth Lester – *Lovin' On Jesus: A Conscise History of Contemporary Worship, 2017*

Les Moir – *Missing Jewel; the Worship Movement that Impacted the Nations*

---

11 For a brief introduction into the Azusa Revival I recommend, Roberts Liardon, The Great Azusa Street Revival, The Life And Sermons Of William Seymour, Embassy Publishing, 2006.

12 Quoted in James S. Stewart, Heralds of God, Charles Scribner's Son, 1946, p.73.

Darrell W. Johnson – *Discipleship on the Edge, An expository journey through the book of Revelation*
Jeremy Riddle – *The Reset*
Ben Lindsay – *We Need To Talk About Race*

Further resources for worship leaders and church leaders:

Worship Central
Worship Central is a global movement of worshippers who long to see the worship of Jesus Christ made central throughout the world. Since launching in 2006, thousands of worship leaders representing over 110 nations have attended the events globally and accessed the resources online.
Worship Central is passionate about developing resources and training opportunities to empower worship leaders among the nations.

- The Podcast, Live Sessions and Course provide free online training and connection with the Worship Central team and global guests.
- Worshippers gather globally at Worship Central Conferences and The Week is a key annual event in the UK, dedicated to developing worship leaders.
- The Academy is a unique and structured opportunity for worship leaders to invest a year in the local church while receiving theological, personal and practical training.
- Worship Central has released five albums; Spirit Break Out, Let It Be Known, Set Apart, Mercy Road and Stir a Passion.

Discover more and get in touch at worshipcentral.org

Tim Hughes – *Passion for Your Name*
Matt Redman – *The Heart of Worship Files*
Matt Boswell (Ed.) – *Doxology and Theology: How the Gospel Forms the Worship Leader*
Bob Kauflin – *Worship Matters*

A. W. Tozer – *Tozer on Worship and Entertainment*, selected excerpts
Podcast: *Resound Worship*
worshipforeveryone.com for inter-generational worship ministry
resources from Nick & Becky Drake
Kingdomworshipmovement.com for resources and retreats
Schoolofworship.org.uk for a one-year course taught on Saturdays,
also accessible by the day
Elimsound.co.uk offers resources and a school of worship
Engageworship.org for resources and training
Creativeexchange.co from Sound of Wales for training
Geraldinelatty.com for singing and choirs
Creativelabacademy.com for music and worship training

SPRING HARVEST · licc · BIBLE STUDIES

essential christian presents

WORSHIPPING

THE GOD OF ALL
IN ALL OF LIFE

EDITED BY
MARK GREENE

Six
studies in
David's
Psalms

Worshipping Edited by Mark Greene

Publishing April 2021

Pre order at: spckpublishing.co.uk/worshipping

Paperback ISBN: 9780281085767   **eBook** ISBN: 9780281086115

https://www.springharvest.org/resources

FINAL COVER COMING SOON

Worship
for
Everyone

WHY ALL-AGE WORSHIP IS IMPORTANT
AND HOW TO MAKE IT WORK

NICK & BECKY DRAKE

Worship For Everyone
Nick Drake & Becky Drake

Publishing May 2021

Pre order at: spckpublishing.co.uk/worship-for-everyone

Paperback ISBN: 9780281085873   **eBook** ISBN: 9780281085880